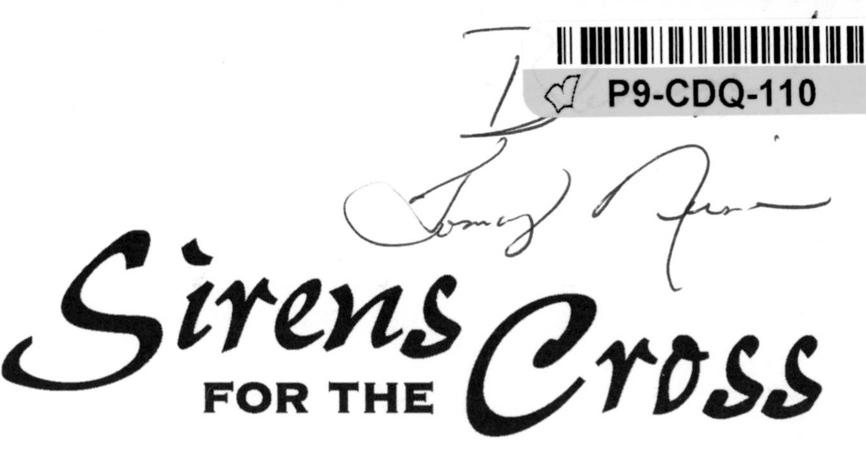

Sirens for the Cross

TOMMY NEIMAN

With

Sue Reynolds

All glory and honor goes to God: The Eternal Rescuer

"For He rescued us from the domain of darkness,
and transferred us to the Kingdom of His beloved Son,
in whom we have redemption, the forgiveness of sins."
Colossians 1: 13-14

First Printing 1998
Second Printing 2000

Published by:
Embrace Communications
6887 Red Mountain Road
Livermore, Colorado 80536

Publisher's Cataloging-in-Publication
(Provided by Quality Books, Inc.)

Neiman, Tommy (Thomas C.), 1962-
Sirens For The Cross / by Tommy Neiman; with Sue Reynolds; editors: Sue Reynolds, Gaius Reynolds, Cherry Sokoloski.
p.cm.
"All glory and honor goes to God: the eternal rescuer."

ISBN: 0-9668878-0-8

1. Fire fighters — Anecdotes. 2. Fire extinction — Religious aspects — Christianity. I. Reynolds, Sue, 1945- II. Reynolds, Gaius. III. Sokoloski, Cherry. IV. Title.

TH9149.N45 1999 363.37 QB198-1702
All scripture excerpts from the New American Standard Version of the Holy Bible unless otherwise noted.

Printed in the United States of America

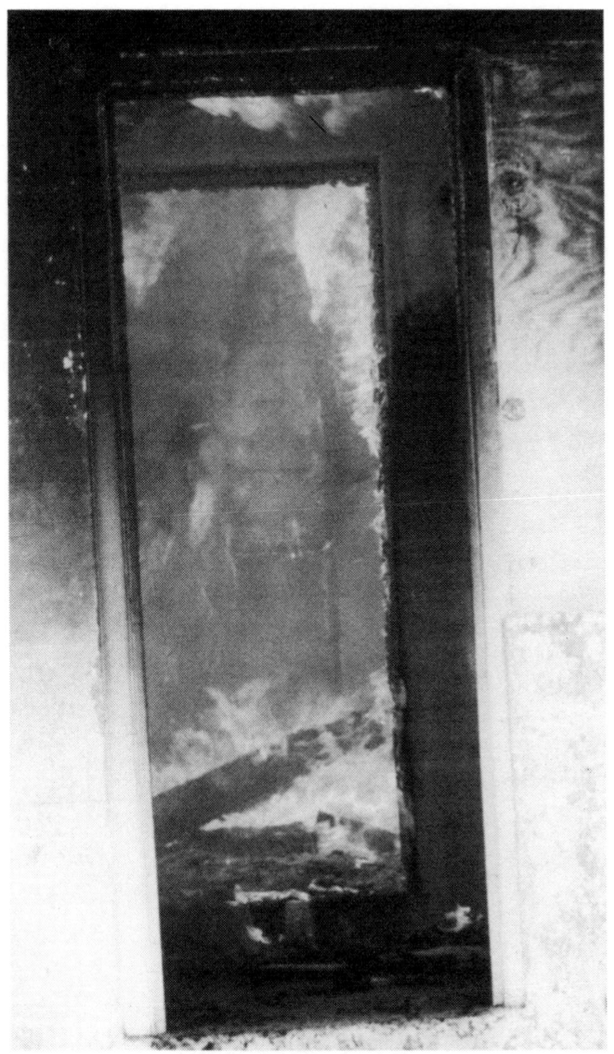

ON THE COVER

Can you see Him in the doorway amidst the flames?

This spiritual, goose-bump inspiring scene is an actual unretouched photo of a burning dwelling used for a training fire.

Many have asked if there was a death or special occurrence in the history of this structure.

The answer is "No!"

This brings us to the conclusion that even in the most ordinary fires — represented by daily trials and struggles — Jesus is right there with us!

ENDORSEMENTS

Those that put themselves in harm's way while responding to urgent calls are true heroes. Firefighters and paramedics have coined a term for that brief window of hope to save lives— 'the golden hour of opportunity.' My friend and active firefighter/paramedic, Tommy Neiman, has captured many of his own 'golden hours of opportunity' in his book **Sirens For The Cross**. *By adding spiritual insights from his evangelical Christian perspective, Tommy focuses on another hour of opportunity, one that has eternal consequences. Challenging and genuinely entertaining reading are within the pages of* **Sirens For The Cross**, *and I highly recommend it.*

JAY STRACK, PRESIDENT AND FOUNDER OF STUDENT LEADERSHIP UNIVERSITY; EXECUTIVE DIRECTOR OF MILLENNIUM CHORUS INTERNATIONAL ORLANDO, FLORIDA.

~

Emergency workers live constantly under a level of uncertainty. I believe Tommy has been given some very special insights into looking at how God works through sometimes terrible situations. There is no stronger force than a person dedicated to helping others in time of need supported by their personal faith. This is a book all Christian Emergency Workers should read. May it be used to strengthen the faith of many.

ED STAUFFER, EXECUTIVE DIRECTOR OF THE FEDERATION OF FIRE CHAPLAINS.

~

This book is a meaningful tool for all of us to use in our everyday life, at the station, and as an effective outreach medium. It reminds us that God is in control, and He does make good out of bad situations. His presence is with us always and He is the Incident Commander at every emergency scene. Read it, share it, and to God be the glory!

GAIUS REYNOLDS, MISSIONARY, FELLOWSHIP OF CHRISTIAN FIREFIGHTERS, INT'L.

ACKNOWLEDGMENTS

A special thanks goes to the men and women of the Saint Lucie County Fire District. You guys are great and even though you have taken to calling me "Rev," Tommy is always willing and ready to listen to whatever is on your heart.

A debt of gratitude goes to my fire department administration not only for providing me with a generous means of supporting my family, but also for an avenue for God to use me to minister to those at the end of the sirens.

To the mission church, Okeechobee Road Baptist, where I serve as pastor and to my home church, Orange Avenue Baptist, thank you for putting up with this "rookie" in the pulpit.

To Gaius Reynolds, missionary and fearless leader of the Fellowship of Christian Firefighters, International, thank you for being a true friend, ever dedicated to seeing God's glory in the Fire Service. "T-man" is always there for you, man.

And finally, this book would not be possible if it weren't for one of God's very special servants, Sue Reynolds. Thank you, Sue, for your continual patience and tireless effort in helping me write this book. You were truly an answer to my prayer for someone to assist me in writing **Sirens For The Cross**. God Bless you.

Sue Reynolds is a freelance writer, speaker, educator, and the editor of **The Encourager,** the publication of the Fellowship of Christian Firefighters, International. She served as Director of Children's Ministries at Calvary Bible Church in Bakersfield, California and has a master's degree in education and a reading specialist credential. Sue and her husband, Gaius, reside in the mountains of Colorado.

Tommy, you are truly one of God's chosen humble servants. It has been a blessing to work with you to bring ***Sirens For The Cross*** *to fruition.*

Sue

The ministry of this book is humbly dedicated to:

First and foremost ~
My Lord and Savior, Jesus Christ. *I love You, Lord.*

Mom ~*for raising me to know the Lord and for your unwavering faith*
&
Dad ~*for your continued growth in love and knowledge of our Lord.*

Robbie and Terry ~ my brothers and fellow pastors.
I knew there was a reason we practiced baptizing each other in the bathtub as toddlers.

Mac and Mae Jean ~
for your loving support and for letting me marry your daughter.

And to a very special blessing from God . . . my family
Alicia ~ God's chosen companion for my life.
Thank you for your unconditional love and continual support. (And for keeping the kids quiet after busy shifts). I love you.

Sara, Luke, and Lauren ~
Thank you for praying for Daddy while he is at work. I love you guys!

Lauren, Tommy, Alicia, Luke, and Sara

CONTENTS

Introduction

" 'For I know the plans I have for you,' declares the Lord, 'plans for welfare and not for calamity to give you a future and a hope . . .' "

JEREMIAH 29:11

Today it's "Rescue 911," "Code 3," "COPS," and "Trauma in the ER." Yesterday, it was Squad 51 of the show "Emergency." "Emergency" was my favorite TV program and I would never miss a Saturday night episode. This show seemed to captivate me as a child. I couldn't get enough of the drama, speeding fire trucks, ambulances, action, quick responses, and realistic heroes in uniform. The intrigue continued into my teenage years. Eventually, armed with a driver's license, I was always on the look out for the flashing lights of emergency vehicles. But, my first passion in life was sports — in particular, baseball. I loved the game, and from childhood through college, baseball was a large part of my life.

It was during my early youth, at nine years of age to be exact, that I experienced God's wonderful saving grace. I trusted Christ as my Savior and Master and prayed that His will for my life was professional baseball. And, indeed, throughout high school and college it appeared that baseball was His will. God gave me continued success until my second year of college when an awkward fall produced a partial dislocation in my shoulder. I didn't want surgery, so the doctor prescribed eight weeks of rest from baseball. I reluctantly retreated to the stands, wishing inwardly that I was still out on the field. My injury lingered well beyond the eight weeks and, for the first time since I was nine, I was filled with doubts. Jeremiah 29:11 says God knows His plans for my life. But it was obvious God's plan and my plan were not one and the same. Doubts filled my mind and all I could do was place everything in His hands.

Within months God began to again heighten my interest in emergency work, especially fire-rescue. I felt Him encouraging me to attend the local college's fire academy. I sensed Him leading me into a part-time hospital security position that provided exposure to the emergency room and rescue personnel in action. The excitement was contagious.

"God, is this what you want me to do?" I began to ask. "Am I competent enough to do this kind of work? Am I capable of handling horrendous accidents that often result in severe injuries, bleeding, loss of limbs, and even death? Will I be able to enter burning buildings and face the possibility of seeing burned bodies? Is this really where you want me, Lord?"

As I prayed and sought God's will, His plan for my life began to unfold. During the summer months, as I worked in the security position, a close friend in the hospital laboratory approached me. "Hey Tommy, there's an opening in the medical examiner's office. Are you interested?"

"Why not?" I figured. "The examiner's office was at the hospital. I could still be around the emergency room and I could always use some extra part-time work. Besides, this could be really interesting."

Interesting doesn't begin to describe what lay ahead. I assumed I would be moving bodies or cleaning equipment. My brothers had worked part-time at funeral homes and that wasn't too bad. This couldn't be much different, could it?

Boy, was I mistaken! The opening was for a denier — a

person who opens up bodies and removes organs during autopsies. The first day on the job I observed an autopsy — sitting down, of course.

"I guess this is as good a time as any to find out if I can handle gory stuff," I thought. Still, I kept asking myself, "What in the world am I doing in here? Should I tell them I'm not interested and leave right now?"

In response, God seemed to say, "Relax, you're not here by mistake."

By His will, I made it through the autopsy and was asked to come back the next day to begin training. I merely nodded my head and left, doubting they would see my face in there again. At least not alive!

I don't remember eating lunch that day — or even dinner, for that matter. But I did go back the next day, praying I would be able to stomach what I was to do and learn what I needed to learn.

God answered those prayers. Within six weeks, and about forty autopsies later, I became the denier for the District 19 medical examiner's office. Over the next year I assisted with over 400 autopsies including some of the most unusual cases an unnatural death can create.

My heart, however, was in fire-rescue. I felt God ultimately leading me in that direction, and wondered why I was working on dead bodies when I was supposed to be learning how to save living ones. I thought I might have been off track and behind schedule in God's plan for my life, but now, as I look back, I know He used the medical examiner's job to teach me several things. First, the ability to handle the extremely horrifying images I would face as a paramedic. Second, the knowledge of human anatomy imperative to getting through paramedic school and treating severely mangled patients. Third, and most overwhelming, that death is real, final, and no respecter of age, position, or person.

The biggest question that plagued me, however, as I opened up those cold, lifeless bodies was, "Did this person know Jesus? Did he or she pass from this life to eternal life with God?"

What about you? If tragedy were to strike you today, do you have the certainty of knowing "that to be absent from the body is to be present with the Lord?" (2 Corinthians 5:8) The scriptures tell us this is possible: "Believe in the Lord Jesus Christ and you will be saved . . ." (Acts 16:31).

God blessed me through the job in the medical examiner's office. Knowing my desire to work in fire-rescue, He gave me the needed confidence and background to get through fire academy and paramedic school. Praise His name!

Today I serve as a full-time firefighter/paramedic with the Fort Pierce/Saint Lucie County Fire District in Fort Pierce, Florida. God has blessed me with a wonderful wife, Alicia, and three wonderful children — Sara, Luke, and Lauren. I have also been blessed in the calling of pastor to a small mission church, Okeechobee Road Baptist Chapel, in the Fort Pierce area. But the most recent burden upon my heart has been to share some of the real situations in which God has been present during the past fourteen years of my career in fire rescue.

The response calls shared in the following pages may resemble scenes from a "Rescue 911" episode, but they vary in one obvious way: these calls all point glory and honor to God! Whether the calls illustrate lessons God revealed or opportunities He provided so I could share His love with others, all praise and honor go to Him.

Many times God's hand on the victim's life is apparent, but His marvels go beyond that. God's handiwork is also evident not only in the life of the rescuer — and I can tell you, He deals with this rescuer a lot.

It is my prayer, as I share some of these dramatic and sometimes tragic situations, that you will be encouraged to see how very real God is, how fragile life is, and most of all, that you will know how critically important it is to know Jesus Christ as your ultimate rescuer.

If you haven't received Christ as your Savior, I encourage you to do so now. Some scriptures to help guide you are found in the conclusion of the final chapter, "The Last Alarm."

CHAPTER 1

The Man Next Door

"Be harmonious, sympathetic, brotherly, kindhearted, and humble in spirit; not returning evil for evil or insult for insult, but giving blessing instead, for you were also called for the very purpose that you might inherit a blessing."

I PETER 3:8-9

I grew up in a pleasant neighborhood in an average, middle-class house with a fenced-in back yard. My first love was base ball. Many days my twin brother, Robbie, and I played baseball in our backyard until the dark of night inhibited our play. Once we tried to rig up lamps and play baseball under the lights.

"Why not?" I reasoned. "They do it all the time on television." Unfortunately, mom's extension cords and lamps wouldn't reach the distance.

I played baseball as many hours a day as possible and was thankful for our fenced-in yard. The fence stopped balls from rolling too far when my brother or I would hit or throw one past the other.

As Robbie and I grew older and our arms became stronger, more and more balls sailed over the fence. When that happened, the ball was usually gone for good. Not because it landed in a pond or got lost in the woods. No! It was gone because it ended up in my neighbor's yard — a place we dared not go!

Our neighbor, Mr. Milner, evoked extreme fear from Robbie

and me. In the eyes of these little ball players, he was the boogie man himself. His house reminded us of the one on the TV show the, "Addams Family." On the front porch was a squeaky iron gate. Near the porch was a concrete goldfish pond with dark, murky, algae-ridden water — monster-ridden too, no doubt. Over the windows were dark blinds that always remained closed. The key inhabitant of the house, Mr. Milner, rarely came outside.

Our first unexpected and frightening encounter with Mr. Milner confirmed our suspicion that he might be the boogie man indeed. Robbie and I were five years old. We had just learned how to climb the fence. We decided to retrieve a baseball that sailed across our fence and into Mr. Milner's yard. Suddenly, a loud scary voice yelled out, "What are you doing? Get out of here!"

The voice came from the very dark screened-in porch.

"Where'd that voice come from?" I said as I jumped so high I probably could have been back over the fence if I'd jumped in the right direction.

We looked around. We saw no one, just a distant shadowy figure behind a mysterious screen door. We hightailed it back over the fence and into our house. Nervously, we looked out our window and watched a very pale, stiff-backed old man emerge from the dark porch, pick up our baseball, and disappear into the black hole again. We knew our baseball was gone for good. And no doubt from that day on, Mr. Milner's baseball collection grew; for after that the thought of ever recovering a baseball or any other sports object which managed to clear the fence was completely abandoned for fear of making contact with him.

Our imaginations, fed by that first encounter, continued to feed our fear. We didn't hate Mr. Milner, we were simply afraid of him — afraid of seeing his angry form descend from that spooky porch and hear his scary voice yell at us. If he had been my little league coach, I'm sure I would have been too afraid to throw anything less than strikes!

Robbie and I quickly adopted one strict rule. If a ball ever went into the boogie man's yard or if he ever appeared, we disappeared. I don't think Mom or Dad grasped the true extent of our fear. They simply passed him off as a grouchy old man who was lonely and had nothing better to do than to yell at kids. Our parents may have been right, but in my young mind I was certain I never wanted to meet him face to face. For the remainder of the time I lived in that neighborhood, I successfully avoided Mr. Milner.

Robbie and I were twelve when our family moved to another part of the city. As the years passed and the struggles of being a teenager began, Mr. Milner slowly faded from my mind. After all, our paths would never cross again — or so I thought.

Fast forward seventeen years, when I was the paramedic on duty at a fire station several miles from my old neighborhood. Our station wasn't the closest to that neighborhood, yet it was the one dispatched to that area on that specific day. I recognized the street name instantly and knew the address was outside our response area. As the tones continued to ring and the dispatcher called out, "a sick person," I was puzzled. "Why are we responding to a call so distant from our station?"

My lieutenant concluded that all the stations in closer proximity were on calls, making us the next closest station able to respond. As the guys began to look at the wall map, I stopped them and said, "Don't bother. I lived on that street for twelve years."

En route, I tried to place in my mind exactly where that particular house was on the street. The dispatcher said the call was for 1608. I knew we had lived at 1606. "It has to be one of the homes next door to our old house," I thought. Then it dawned on me, it could be the old "Addam's Family" house. My childhood anxieties and fears resurfaced. A mild panic gripped my mind. I felt like a five-year-old kid again, riddled with fear.

"This is silly," I said to myself. "Calm down. It's probably the house on the other side, and even if it is Mr. Milner's old place he most likely isn't there anymore." I rationalized, " Maybe he died years ago. He was old, and seventeen years have passed."

My heart skipped when I looked out the ambulance window and realized which way the numbers ran on the street. No doubt about it. We were going to Mr. Milner's house.

"What if he's still living? What if he's still in that same house? Even worse, what if he is the one we are responding to?"

Oh, boy! I pictured entering the house. I imagined hearing that chilling voice say, "You, a paramedic? Get out of here. Now I really am sick!"

Remarkably, as my anxieties reached their peak, a calming peace came over me. I realized the Holy Spirit was quietly reassuring me and allowing me to see that I was going there for a purpose. God's mighty hand was in this and there were no reasons for doubt or fear. No other peace can compare to the beautiful peace the Holy Spirit bestows in the most doubt-ridden times. It was in the midst of this warm spiritual assurance that I realized I could soon be facing the boogie man from my past.

The street seemed shorter than I remembered. The houses appeared smaller. We slowed down just past my old house. We stopped right in front of Mr. Milner's place. As we exited the rescue truck I told the other guys, "I might know this person." I pointed to the house next door and said, "That's the house I grew up in."

I grabbed my equipment and headed toward that iron gate. I whispered, "Lord, you are in control."

I pulled my hat down a little lower than normal. Glancing into my old yard, I felt as if I were looking through a scrapbook of memories.

I pulled my hat down a little lower than normal. Glancing into my old yard, I felt as if I were looking through a scrapbook of memories. There was the carport where we'd often roller-skated, our favorite climbing tree, my old bedroom window from which I would vacantly stare on rainy days, and of course, the fenced-in backyard. Everything seemed to have shrunk. The world is definitely bigger through the eyes of a child.

We opened the squeaky iron gate. It was only waist high — and not nearly as intimidating as I remembered it. I glanced at the old concrete goldfish pond realizing the Loch Ness monster did not reside there and never had — except in my imagination.

The final moment of truth approached. The door opened revealing a much older Mrs. Milner.

"What's going on today?" I cautiously asked while looking for any sign of recognition from her.

"My husband is very ill," she anxiously said while holding the door open for us to enter.

She didn't seem to recognize me as I entered her home, a place I'd lived close to for twelve years, had feared since I was five, and had never been inside of. I looked about the room, half expecting to see a big crate of old baseballs in some corner. Instead I saw a home filled with solemn family members. I closed the door.

"Where is our patient?" I asked.

She pointed toward a back bedroom.

I considered maintaining my anonymity. I could just slide through this call and be on my way. Besides, if Mr. Milner was sick, my identity might only make things worse. I immediately realized Satan's handiwork and his cop-out voice in my ear.

Mrs. Milner informed me of the severity of her husband's illness. I began to tremble inside as I heard her say, cancer. The cancer, she explained was in its advanced stage and had spread throughout his body.

I was still scared, but I knew God was in control. I entered the room to gaze upon a feeble, shriveled Mr. Milner, a man unrecognizable as the monster I had envisioned him to be as a child. I approached his frail, ashen body and gently shook this shadow of my former neighbor. His eyes barely opened. I knew his hours left on earth were few. At that moment, the magnitude of God's divine appointment struck me hard. "Lord, this is so powerful, so awesome," I thought to myself. Barely breathing and nearly unconscious, he made futile attempts to open his eyes. His gaunt face and visibly protruding bones suggested he would soon be gone from this life. I moved to his side and felt a weak pulse through a cold wrist.

Mrs. Milner continued to relate a litany of information, including the severity of pain her husband had experienced along with the physician's suggestion that Mr. Milner be transported to the emergency room to receive comfort medication.

We had the option to summon a non-emergency private ambulance to handle the transport, but I knew this was one ambulance ride God wanted me to take. True, this was not a physical emergency, but God deemed it a spiritual emergency.

I crouched down to Mr. Milner's ear. "We are with fire-rescue. We will be taking you to the hospital."

While one of our guys went to get the stretcher, Mrs. Milner reaffirmed the "do not resuscitate" orders lying on the table beside his bed. I assured her we would honor those wishes. As we lifted his nearly weightless body onto the stretcher, I sensed God leading me to allow the others to wheel Mr. Milner on ahead to the truck while I sought Mrs. Milner's attention.

"We will take good care of your husband," I said. "You know, I'm one of the twins that grew up next door," I added meekly.

She looked closely at me and gave me a surprised, yet gentle smile. Recognition beamed on her face. I felt a loving acceptance replace my once smothering fear. Maybe in that smile she was also able to momentarily reflect on younger, brighter, healthier days.

With that little blessing, I left for the truck praying for the opportunity to be a blessing to a dying man.

We had only a short trip. Using the hand-held telemetry

phone to contact the emergency room, I quickly transmitted a brief patient assessment to the emergency room physician. After hanging up, I looked out the window. The hospital was only a block away. "Lord, I need time with this man," I thought.

I was about to get rattled when I heard the voice of the Holy Spirit say, "Just trust me."

We wheeled Mr. Milner into treatment room number four. We transferred his weak, pain-ridden body to the hospital bed. As I was raising the safety rails on the bed, the nurse at the desk told me to close the treatment area curtain and that she would be in shortly to give him his medication. I abandoned the usual paperwork and used this God-given opportunity to share some final moments with Mr. Milner.

"Go on ahead," I told my guys as I retreated behind the curtain and over to Mr. Milner's side. A precious few moments were granted us and I wasn't about to miss this opportunity. I took hold of Mr. Milner's hand and told him who I was. I shared salvation through Jesus Christ. I told him how he could spend eternity in God's mighty hands. I informed him it was never too late and that acceptance could be done without a spoken word. He simply needed to believe and trust Jesus to come into his heart.

"Do you believe that Jesus is God's Only Son and that He loves you and died for your sins?" I asked.

He squeezed my hand.

"Do you believe and trust Jesus to be your own personal Savior?"

He squeezed my hand once more.

I caressed his hand with both of mine. I told him his pain would soon be over and I would see him later — in eternity.

I stepped from behind that curtain spiritually enlightened. I had no desire to do my earthly report. I just wanted to bask in God's miracle.

In medical terms, this was a Code 1 call: no lights and no sirens. In spiritual terms it was a Code 3, for the Sirens for the

Cross were blaring in my heart. For forty-five minutes that day God turned a "sick person" call into one of the most exciting calls of my career, a call that changed my heart about my childhood nemesis and changed my expectations of future calls forever.

God's handiwork made possible the acceptance of one more into His kingdom. Once again God's Word proved true. "Do not return evil for evil or insult for insult, . . . for you were called for the very purpose that you might inherit a blessing."

CHAPTER 2

Let The Blood Flow

"For God so loved the World that He gave His only begotten Son, that whoever believes in Him shall not perish, but have eternal life . . ."

JOHN 3:16

Let the blood flow! Does this sound gross to you? Does it trigger thoughts of an impending story of a gory rescue call? Unfortunately, the details of this call aren't exactly pretty, but the whole scenario serves as a reminder of the unfathomable love of God. Let me explain.

It was a hot summer Saturday night during my rookie year on the fire department. I was a new, gung ho paramedic ready to treat whatever came my way. I was stationed in a high crime and violence area — an area prone to daily medical calls involving trauma. A call came in merely stating, "a woman bleeding." The location was a street corner near a telephone booth in the heart of the worst part of town. As a rookie and the third man on the team, I rode in the back of the truck which gave me a complete perspective of the surroundings. I was intrigued by the reactions of the people on the streets — reactions that ranged from excitement and thrill at hearing the sirens and seeing the bright lights, to total indifference. We whirled by areas filled with condemned and recently burned buildings, clubs, bars, and street corner hang outs. We rolled into a neighborhood noted for prostitution, drug abuse and dealing, and drive-by shootings. Nothing was safe in this part of town, including our rescue vehicle.

When we arrived on scene, we found exactly what the dispatcher described — "a woman bleeding." But this woman — was in an unusual predicament. She was cradled in the arms of a huge man.

We looked all around, and began a scene size up. I approached cautiously. My first impression was positive. It appeared that the man was holding her until help arrived. I moved nearer to the man. A closer look told me my initial assessment was incorrect. He wasn't holding her — he was restraining her. The woman was semi-conscious and moaning. Knife slashes covered her body. The warm night air was permeated with the smell of blood. My senses heightened. I took an even closer look at the man's facial expressions and gestures. This giant of a man, restraining this bloody woman, obviously had a mental disability. His words were slow and deliberate, his movements sluggish and uncoordinated, and his eyes, set deep in a Mongoloid face, emitted a look of commitment to hold and protect this woman. I looked directly into his eyes and perceived a gentle giant: a kind man who appeared content to bear-hug this woman. Yet, something was amiss. This gentle giant seemed disturbed and irrational.

Knife slashes covered her body. The warm night air was permeated with the smell of blood. My senses heightened.

"What's going on, man?" I asked in the direction of the six-and-one-half foot, 300 plus pounds mountain of a guy.

My suspicion of mental inadequacy was confirmed. Without looking up, and tightening his hug on the woman, he began to chant, "Let the blood flow, let the blood flow."

"Central, get the police department out here immediately,"

my lieutenant called in on his portable radio.

Despite my lieutenant's urgent plea for help, I feared it would be a long time before the police would arrive. Crime activity was high that night and calls were backed up. "If only 911 would have known the details of this," I thought.

This lady was losing more blood with each second. Knife-like incisions covered her face and arms. Deep slashes in her T-shirt revealed deep cuts across her upper torso. Her hair was matted and bloody, giving the impression that her assailant had relentlessly hacked away at her in a repeated slicing fashion. She needed to get to a hospital — and fast — but not attached to some guy the size of a Dallas Cowboy lineman.

We continued to wait anxiously, yet helplessly, for the police to arrive. We tried to talk some sense into this guy. We attempted — unsuccessfully — to talk him into letting the lady go.

A crowd of bystanders grew. They too pleaded for him to let go of her. As a couple of well-meaning people tried to pull the bleeding woman from the determined man's arms, he calmly, yet effortlessly, pushed them away. All this time he continued chanting, "Let the blood flow, let the blood flow."

One of the bystanders jumped on the man's broad back in an attempt to separate him from the woman. The captor never loosened his stronghold. He merely wiggled his shoulders, easily maneuvering the good Samaritan off his back.

His cries filled the night air, "Let the blood flow, it's comin' from her heart, the blood has to flow, just let it flow, let it flow, let it flow . . ."

Never once did the man look at anyone around him. He was in his own world, out of tune with those around him, and he was keeping medical attention from a badly bleeding lady.

As we waited, our minds raced. Had this giant inflicted the wounds? If so, Why? What could cause a man to be so violent and now equally overprotective to the point of further endangering this woman's life?

It seemed forever, but in reality it was only a minute or so before two officers arrived. Instantly they sized up the situation, then demanded, "Let the lady go!"

Ignoring the command, the man continued to chant, "Let the blood flow."

The officers went into action. The larger of the two officers stood at least six feet four inches tall. Even at that he looked like a dwarf next to the giant. He walked around the man. The other officer kept him facing us. Then the bigger officer took his baton. He motioned for us and his partner to grab the bleeding woman's arms. The very second we latched onto her, the officer behind the giant made a quick placement of the baton around his neck. He jerked the huge man to the ground. So great was the impact that it felt as if the pavement moved when he struck the ground. The woman literally fell into our arms. Nearly unconscious from the large amount of blood loss, she lay lifelessly in our grasp.

Now it was our time to go into action. We carried her into the truck and placed her on the stretcher. We began throwing pressure gauzes on her multiple, bleeding lacerations. That accomplished, I checked her blood pressure. It barely registered.

Without a moment to lose, my lieutenant hit the pedal and we were off. The sirens roared and the lights flashed as we hurried toward the hospital. While en route, we pumped large amounts of fluid through IV's and oxygenated her with 100% high flow oxygen to keep her from going further into shock. In an effort to keep her blood perfusing to the vital organs of her body, we placed her in a trendelenberg, or shock position, by elevating her legs and feet.

At the hospital, the emergency room staff took over. Hundreds of stitches and extensive treatment followed. Through the mighty hand of God, this woman survived.

In the aftermath, we discovered this woman had been knifed by another man, not the giant who clung to her at the scene. Incredibly, she made her way to the phone booth at the intersection and called 911. She said she needed an ambulance because she was bleeding, then hung up. Evidently that's where her captor came across her.

For months I wondered how a person could just let another person bleed like that. Then I heard someone retell the story of Jesus' death on the cross.

God, Jesus' own Father, forsook His Son on the cross. Jesus' Father let the blood of His own Son flow.

My mind flashed back to that night when the big guy kept saying, "Let the blood flow, let blood flow, let the blood flow." I recalled the horrible sight of that lady's blood pouring from her body as we stood by helplessly. Then I thought about Christ's precious blood flowing from his maimed body and how His Father refused to stop it — refused because He loved us so very much. Jesus' blood had to flow to cleanse us and make us whole. In essence God said, "Let the blood flow."

What a horrible sight it must have been that day for those who loved Jesus. What pain and helplessness they must have felt as they watched soldiers nail Him to an old, splintered cross. What agony must have plagued them as His mangled, beaten body was raised up to bleed to death in front of their very eyes.

May our eyes and hearts never take lightly the blood that flowed from Calvary that day nearly 2000 years ago when God said, "Let the blood flow!" May we always remember that God loved us so much that He sent Jesus to die on the cross so we can spend eternity with Him in heaven.

A LIGHTER MOMENT

"There is an appointed time for everything . . ."

Going Backwards

Running around with flashing lights and sirens, going through red lights, and driving down center lanes of traffic at excessively high speeds, can be exciting. It wasn't the reason I got into fire-rescue, but it was an added thrill. I even worked on my days off with a private ambulance company that would occasionally run lights and sirens. I was "ate up" with this kind of excitement. However, two incidents occurred in my rookie year that opened my eyes to the seriousness of operating emergency vehicles. In retrospect they are humorous, but at the time the results could have been tragic.

The first occurred on my third shift of duty. I was fulfilling the departmental policy of driving the ambulance on five supervised rescue calls before becoming eligible to be checked off in all the department's vehicles. The call came in around 7:00 p.m. as a traffic accident. My heart raced as I drove the ambulance, complete with lights and sirens, to the scene. The accident was minor but this was early in my career and any call, especially a car wreck, was pulse-pounding for me. We pulled ahead of the cars involved, slammed on the brakes, jumped out of our truck, and briskly walked to the scene. As I walked toward the scene, I intuitively glanced back at the ambulance.

The truck was moving, and it was moving right toward us!

I looked for my ambulance partners. They were both with me.

"Oh no!" I hollered as three sets of eyes immediately doubled in size.

The truck was in reverse! Not a good move on my part. Fortunately, it had a slow transmission, so it had slowly started moving — but not only was it moving right toward us, it was also moving toward the two accident vehicles.

I ran as fast as I could, got the door open, and slammed down the brake. A precious few feet remained between the heavy rescue truck and the closest vehicle in which the victim was still seated — wide-eyed and thankful not be a victim twice in the same day.

The second incident occurred during an out-of-town transport while I was driving for a private ambulance company. We were transporting an older, senile gentleman to a hospital in Miami. He had multiple health problems — heart, breathing, you name it — coupled with severe mental illness. The trip proceeded smoothly, until we reached the outer city limits of Miami.

I was driving. My partner was tending to our patient in the back of the truck. Suddenly, without warning, a motorist several cars ahead stopped his car abruptly on the interstate, causing a chain reaction. The car ahead of me struck the car ahead of it. We were the next in line and destined to impact the car in front of us! My brakes locked. Miraculously, in the skid, the Lord guided that large ambulance just to the right of the car ahead that had already struck another car.

But wait! We weren't through skidding. Instead, we hit a guard rail at just the right angle to cause our ambulance to roll over on its side. I looked out my driver's side window at the fine pieces of gravel in the highway asphalt. My mind went into a blur.

"Are you all right?" my partner asked.

"Yeah! What about the patient?" I replied, tilting my head up and looking through to the back.

"He's okay!" my partner said. "Look at him."

What I saw caused me to briefly chuckle. Our patient, locked-in and seat-belted securely, was lying sideways on the stretcher and smiling ear to ear.

"Are we there yet?" he asked.

"No, not yet," I said. "But you will get there soon. And you know what? You're gonna get to ride in another ambulance today!"

"All right," he cheerfully said.

A crew from Miami fire-rescue arrived, opened our back door, and asked if we were all right. After our affirmative reply, they took our patient and my partner to our intended hospital.

Within moments the media converged on the scene. After one television interview, I took refuge from the other reporters in the front seat of a highway patrol vehicle. I sat there watching the highway patrol officers do their reports and measure tire marks. "My career is done." I thought. "There will probably be ten lawyers hunting our patient down, wanting to help him sue me and this ambulance company."

Thanks to God, the highway patrolman's report stated I was not at fault and should, in fact, be commended for not smashing our heavy ambulance into the car ahead of me.

The patrolman drove me to the hospital to meet our patient and my partner. I walked into the psychological medical area where the patient was transferred. And sure enough, there were already two men in nice suits talking to him. The interstate ambulance roll-over had hit the midday news! I walked across the lobby. A frustrated look covered the two legal faces standing before our patient.

"How are you doing?" I asked encouragingly, placing my hand on the patient's shoulder.

"Great," he said as he smiled. "Are you taking me somewhere?"

"No, this place is where you'll be for awhile," I said.

Just then one of those annoying legal faces cut in and captured the patient's attention. "Sir — um, sir? Will you please try to concentrate a moment. Do you remember the accident today? Can you explain what happened?"

"Absolutely," our patient said. "You see, the accident was out on the battlefield. I was lying low in a foxhole and. . . ."

I smiled, and walked away.

God sure gave us the right kind of patient that day.

". . . A time to laugh."

ECCLESIASTES 3A: 1 AND 4B

CHAPTER 3

The Cactus Guy

"I will say to the Lord, 'My refuge and my fortress, My God in whom I trust!' For it is He who delivers you from the snare of the trapper and from the deadly pestilence."

PSALM 91:2-3

Backdraft explosions, collapsing structures, entrapment in burning buildings, hazardous exposure — there seems to be no end to the dangers in the job of fire-rescue.

In recent years, communicable diseases emerged as a major concern and potentially life-threatening danger in the rescue profession. The mere mention of AIDS evokes instant fear and apprehension, and rightfully so — you get it, and you're dead! Perhaps not instantly, but you will die!

Training that continually stresses the danger of Aids points out the fact that it can be transmitted from a needle stick. This is an unnerving thought, especially in my profession, where I am often required to stick needles into unpredictable people in dark alleys or dimly lit rooms.

When responding to a call where there is risk of contracting this deadly disease, it is imperative to use all medical precautions available, especially when that call is in an area noted for drug abuse, prostitution, and high-risk diseases. Rescue workers are trained to continually maintain barriers such as a gown, mask, and latex gloves between their exposed skin and the fluids or broken skin of any patient encountered. The full body gowns, carried in most rescue vehicles today, were not yet available on the following call. However, at times even the most advanced medical precautions are inadequate and the best armor is the power of prayer. Such was the situation in the case I call "The Cactus Guy."

About 3:00 p.m., on a very warm summer day, a call came in merely stating, "a fall with a cut". Nothing special, scary, or intriguing about this call. In fact, while en route, I envisioned the usual scenario of an older person who slipped and fell in the bathroom, perhaps hitting his head on the sink or toilet. But this turned out to be far from the usual "Help! I've fallen and I can't get up" call!

Since details were unavailable, we responded Code 3 with lights and sirens — and thankfully so, as precious seconds were ticking away for this patient.

It was an uneventful trip to our destination, but when the driver and assistant — both EMT's — and I pulled up to the address, caution signs immediately welled within us. This lower middle class neighborhood was well-maintained except for this particular house that was unkempt and run-down. A heightened awareness made me aware that the odor reaching my nostrils was distinctly drug filled. Music continued to blare and several people continued to party despite the injured victim's dire condition. Others were crowding around the door. Distraught expressions covered their faces. Hands waved frantically, motioning us to hurry.

Wasting no time, we grabbed our trauma bags. We rushed toward the gathering crowd. Halfway there I noticed a figure lying in their midst. My adrenaline began to flow. This was not an ordinary figure, but a bright red figure. The closer I got, the more red I saw. The patient was totally covered with bright red blood, indicating the bleeding was coming from an artery. Arteries, the first vessels blood is pumped into as it leaves the heart, have strong walls that hold the blood under high pressure. Consequently, bleeding from an artery is frequently rapid and profuse, and blood literally spurts with each heart beat. There was no doubt that this injury was of a serious nature. My expression must have conveyed concern.

"He fell through the front door," a bystander frantically yelled out.

I glanced up. The front door was partly open. I took a quick step to my left to get a closer look at the door's side. The huge glass window in the middle of the door was broken off at knee level. The jagged edge, still bloody from the twenty-eight-year-old man who had crashed through it moments earlier, looked treacherous. It was an unbelievable sight.

"What happened?" I inquired of no one in particular.

The smell of alcohol filled the air. Someone attempted to explain. "This guy and his friends have been drinking all morning — and a lot."

Another added, "Yeah he was just standing inside the house near the front door with a drink in his hand when he stumbled. I saw him lose control and crash backward through that large glass window in the front door. Then the door flew open. The back of his legs were caught and hanging on the edge of the window where the glass had broken. Then, like a sling shot, he went flying off the glass, slicing deep cuts through the backs of his legs."

We examined the scene. It was apparent that the outward momentum of the door threw the man off the razor-sharp jagged edge into, of all things, a large cactus planter to the side of the front door.

My mind raced. Alcohol and drugs frequently go hand in hand. I gazed at the blood-ridden man. I scanned his body for the places that were bleeding the most. We had to act fast. No time to worry about a potentially deadly transmitted disease. His consciousness was rapidly decreasing. I was sure his blood pressure was doing likewise. I shot God one of those "arrow prayers" as I grabbed two trauma towels and stepped carefully into the six-inch-high cactus planter where the bulk of his body lay. Kneeling down, I saw hundreds of yellow cactus slivers penetrating his flesh. As I put on latex gloves, the haunting thought hit me that these were the only armor I had against an assault of stickers both on him and around me. How horrifyingly easy it would be for bloody cactus stickers to quickly transmit any potentially deadly diseases into my blood stream. But there was no time to contemplate that. This guy was bleeding to death and I needed to move fast. My faith was put to the test. I had to trust the Lord and press on with the job at hand.

Further examination revealed that the glass door edge had sliced nearly all the way through the backs of his legs to the kneecaps. Blood literally poured from the large exposed vessels into the cactus foliage underneath him. Exposed muscles, tendons, arteries, shredded tissue and ligaments were further indicators of the life-threatening seriousness of his injuries. I quickly stuffed trauma dressings into both gashes behind his knees. I bent his legs up to try to stop the blood flow. Wasting no time, my partner and I threw trauma gauze on numerous lacerations all over his body. I glanced at my hands. The latex gloves were completely red and shiny from his blood and my sweat. But the work was only beginning. We had to free him from that cactus. We must transport him — and soon.

As with any fall when a spinal injury is suspected, proper precautions must be heeded. Stabilize his cervical spine. Apply the C-collar. Maintain manual stabilization. Place him on the rigid backboard — not an easy task. This meant logrolling him onto his side to get the board into position. Even with utmost care, there was no way to avoid the consequence of more cactus splinters for him. It also presented the potential for cactus splinters in me as I cleared the large cactus pieces embedded in his back. Another "arrow prayer."

As we logrolled him onto his left side, he shrieked with pain. I removed his blood-soaked shirt. The cactus pieces embedded in the shirt and his back came loose. His bare skin was loaded with gobs of those sharp, piercing, minute, yellow cactus splinters. I removed as many as possible, but still there was no choice but to lay him cautiously on the backboard with hundreds of cactus splinters still embedded in his raw flesh. I couldn't imagine that pain coupled with the pain of having cactus stickers on the insides of large open lacerations. If there was any advantage to his decreased level of consciousness, it was in the fact that consciousness to the intensity of pain also lessened.

I began to lose my focus. "How many of those cactus splinters penetrated my gloves?" I wondered.

No time for such thoughts. My partner and I lifted the board from the planter. We placed the man on the stretcher. The white gauze and trauma towels under his knees were turning red. He was losing more and more consciousness causing his pain to subside even more. We couldn't let him drift into unconsciousness for fear we would not be able to revive him.

"Hey buddy," I pleaded. "Stay awake. Stay with us now, man."

He looked at us with a pale face and lifeless stare as he uttered half sentences. We wheeled him to the truck, all the time trying to keep him alert. I stuffed another towel under his legs in an attempt to stay the rapid hemorrhaging.

While glancing at the sight behind us of broken glass in the huge pool of blood in the cactus planter, I thought, "What a bloody mess!" I looked back at our patient. "This guy is bad. I hope we didn't endanger our lives for naught."

Once in the ambulance, I threw on the blood pressure cuff. The reading was well under 100. My suspicions were confirmed — Impending shock. With a maximum flow of oxygen through a mask, I elected to go ahead with the application of the military anti-shock garment or mast suit. This inflatable lower body garment would hopefully apply significant pressure to those life-threatening lacerations that nearly severed his legs, keep the pressure dressings in place, assist in keeping this man from going into shock from blood loss, and help keep the pressure flow intact to the vital organs such as his brain, lungs, kidney, and heart. We wasted no time. Within three minutes we had the garment on and one large-bore IV established with the maximum amount of fluid infusing.

"Time to roll!" I yelled to our driver.

Just then the back door opened. "I want to go, I'm his girlfriend," a panicky girl demanded. She stepped into the truck.

Protocol demands that family and loved ones ride up front with the driver, but time was too important an issue. I conceded to her wishes and quickly slammed the back door closed behind her.

"Go!" I yelled again.

"You're gonna have to sit down on the bench seat and put your seat belt on," I hurriedly told her as we pulled off.

Stunned, she obediently complied.

I grabbed another bag of fluid, drip hook-up, large needle, and macro drip tubing for a second large-bore IV. "This gal is really going to freak if this guy goes straight-line," I thought as I spiked the bag with the IV tubing. I prayed, "Lord, please don't let him die."

The ride to the hospital would take at least seven or eight minutes. It was imperative to get as much fluid as possible into the patient to keep him from going into shock. Grabbing his other arm and feeling carefully around the many small cactus slivers for an accessible vein, I threw on a constricting band. Locating a vein was a challenge. His arm was literally covered with cactus splinters. His blood pressure was low, making the veins small and difficult to locate. I tightened the band and prayed. As I tried to locate a vein for inserting the IV, I couldn't help but think that there must be a number of those little pokers in me that I didn't even know about. Could I be receiving direct blood-to-blood contact and possibly contract a communicable disease, perhaps a deadly one? It was a chilling thought. Miraculously, I found a vein, injected the large needle, and established a second IV.

In hopes of bringing up his deathly low blood pressure, I

began flowing the maximum amount of IV fluid, sodium chloride, into his system. The first IV bag was nearly empty. Time for another set of vital signs. All right! His blood pressure was over 100.

"Great," I thought. "He's responding to the fluid replacement." But his level of consciousness was still depressed. He was moaning, and only opened his eyes momentarily when spoken to. I was not able to illicit a verbal response even in his dreadfully painful situation. Despite improved vital signs, unconsciousness seemed imminent. Thank God the emergency room was only minutes away.

Quickly I encoded the patient findings to the base hospital physician. "We have a suspected priority one trauma patient with a decreased level of consciousness and serious arterial bleeding in the lower extremities."

They assured me they were prepared and standing by.

We headed directly to the hospital's trauma treatment area where he would receive further stabilization efforts prior to surgical intervention.

As we pulled up to the hospital, his girlfriend, who had remained remarkably cool during the trip, began to cry, "Is he going to make it?"

"We're doing everything we can," I told her. "You just have to trust the Lord!"

She nodded her head in agreement as I opened the back door.

Wheeling the patient into the emergency room, those words, "You just have to trust God," echoed in my head. I realized how much I needed to trust the Lord. "You better practice what you preach, Tommy."

Fear continued to invade my peace. In a few short minutes I would find out how many of those little yellow pokes I had inherited from that cactus guy!

We wheeled him into the trauma room. Several nurses and the doctor helped us move him onto the hospital gurney. I gave

I noticed some small holes in the cuffs of the gloves. The moment of truth arrived.

them a brief rundown on his latest condition and headed for the report room — not to immediately do my report, but to inspect myself for cactus splinters.

I carefully removed my gloves. Normally, they go directly into the bio-waste bin in the treatment area. Not this time — not before a long close look to see how many of those little guys were stuck in those bloody latex gloves. I noticed some small holes in the cuffs of the gloves. I took a deep breath. The moment of truth arrived. I held my hands up to the fluorescent light. Turning my hands at angles and checking for anything that would be protruding, I could not find one single cactus sliver embedded in my hands or in the bloody gloves. Next I examined my bloody sweaty arms. Praise the Lord! I found absolutely nothing. I turned to my partner. A smile covered his face. He too came up cactus-free. AMEN!

Excited at the findings, I looked over at him and said, "God was sure looking over and protecting us today, wasn't he?" My partner nodded emphatically in agreement. "You're not kiddin, Tommy."

How miraculous are God's ways! How great is His concern for us! How truthful is His word! In Psalm 91:2-3 David speaks of God in the following way: " 'My refuge and my fortress, My God in whom I trust!' For it is He who delivers you from the snare of the trapper and from the deadly pestilence."

On that hot, muggy, summer afternoon, God's word was truly my fortress. He did indeed save me from a potentially deadly pestilence.

Our patient, the cactus guy, underwent extensive reconstructive surgery and eventually recovered. I don't think he will ever know how the Lord used his accident to strengthen the faith of this paramedic. Praise God, for "He watcheth over me."

A LIGHTER MOMENT

"There is an appointed time for everything . . ."

Out With The Old In With The New

Out with the old, in with the new. This describes the back-to-back rescue calls I received one Friday afternoon.

The first call came in as a "fall." We arrived to find an elderly gentleman sitting in a lawn chair in the midst of several family members and friends. He had a homemade ice pack cooling down a pretty good bump on the side of his head. He was awake and talkative — complaining to his family for calling 911.

"We just want to make sure you're OK," they told him. And he was. But the unique thing was the occasion for this get-together of friends and family. It was this gentleman's 107th birthday! And he had fallen while dancing around the swimming pool!

We headed back for the truck, talking about how neat it must be to be able to dance at the age of 107.

The next call came less than two hours later: "a woman in labor."

We arrived to find a young lady experiencing occasional labor contractions. She was in her ninth month and within a day of her due date. I explained to her excited husband and parents that since the contractions were rather far apart, the bag of water had not ruptured, and there was no sign of a baby's head in the birth canal, it might be a little while before the arrival of the couple's first child.

Since we were there already, I asked the guys to get the stretcher. I told the expectant mom we would transport her to the hospital.

As the guys retrieved the stretcher, our mother-to-be had a very strong contraction. It was strong enough to give me an eerie feeling that something might be happening. I rechecked her. Her bag of water ruptured and that's not all — a little head started to emerge.

"Forget the stretcher! Get my OB kit," I yelled.

Excitement resurfaced as family members gathered around. I gowned-out and two contractions later, God's beautiful gift of a human life slid into my hands.

How great is God's gift of life, whether 107 years old or one second young.

". . . A time to laugh."

ECCLESIASTES 3A: 1 AND 4B

CHAPTER 4

A Leap Of Faith

"The steps of a man are established by the Lord, and He delights in his ways. When he falls, he shall not be hurled headlong, because the Lord is the One who holds his hand."

PSALM 37: 23-24

Allen was a frustrated young man. He had lost all hope of finding meaning or happiness in life. He held a master's degree, yet he was discouraged in his career. His friends and family loved him, yet he felt lonely and confused. Allen was fed up with his life, he had no vision for his future, and no desire to continue life's journey. He was ready to check out. So, that's exactly what he decided to do.

He obtained a gun and some shells, loaded the gun, climbed into his car, and headed out to find a good place to kill himself. Fearing the possibility of a family member having to see and identify his body, he decided to head north and far away from his Miami apartment. His mind was made up.

That same morning, my shift was ending and I was looking forward to going home when the station phone rang. I answered.

"Hey Tommy!" the oncoming shift supervisor said. "How about some overtime at another station?"

"Which one?"

"Station 8," he said.

"Station 8?" I thought to myself. "That station is as far south as our county goes — no way."

I politely declined the offer but reluctantly agreed to take it if they couldn't find another paramedic. I hung up and hastily gathered my personal gear, hoping to make it to my truck before they called back. I was nearly out the door.

The phone rang again. "It's for you, Tommy."

"Oh no," I thought as I went to the phone. "I'd better pack my uniform."

"Tommy, this is David French" my next door neighbor and a fellow paramedic said. "I'll take half the overtime at Station 8 if you take the other half."

"I just told them no, David," I said.

"Come on, Tommy," he pleaded. "I'll do the night half if you'll do the day."

I reluctantly agreed, packed my gear, and headed for the station. This particular station was a one-half hour drive down the intracoastal waterway. I'd been there only once about three years ago, when I worked a shift swap with another firefighter. As I drove to the station I wondered, "Why did I even agree to this? Wait 'till I get my hands on David French!"

I pulled into Station 8, unloaded my bunker gear, and settled in for what would hopefully be an uneventful twelve hours.

Meanwhile, Allen continued his quest north from Miami along the intracoastal waterway in search of somewhere to stop and take his life. He passed town after town and city after city. He was almost 100 miles up the coast from Miami. He stopped his car.

"I've driven far enough. I've thought long enough. Nothing matters. This is as good a place as any," he said to himself.

He looked around. He was in a semi-vacant condominium parking lot in the response zone of — you guessed it —Station 8.

He grabbed the gun, jammed the shell in, and cocked the trigger.

"Click!"

"What's wrong with this thing?" he cried out in exasperation.

He cocked the trigger again. Once again he put the gun to his head.

"Click!"

Nothing happened. "I can't even kill myself right!"

Disgusted, he looked at the adjacent building. Realizing suicide at gunpoint was not working, and determined to carry out his mission, he decided to jump off the building. He got out of his car, walked through the lobby, and hit the top floor button after entering the elevator. The door closed, and Allen was on his way. But the elevator suddenly stopped at the seventh floor. The door opened, leaving Allen confronted with residents waiting to enter. Not wanting his unfamiliar face to cause suspicion and possibly thwart his goal, Allen figured he was up high enough and quickly exited the elevator.

He headed down the hallway to the end of the balcony, climbed over the railing, closed his eyes, and jumped.

Back at Station 8, I was reading the sports page. Our station tones sounded. The call came in as "a fall at a condo." Since most of the condos in the area were occupied by retired folks, I thought it was just one of those normal, "I've fallen and I can't get up" calls. Most of them are, and I had no reason to believe otherwise. Nonetheless, since detailed information was unavailable, we ran our normal response with lights and sirens.

When we arrived at the scene, we were once again reminded to always expect and prepare for the worst. Before us was not a little old lady who slipped and fell in the lobby, but Allen, a young man sprawled out on the asphalt pavement. His mangled legs, from his mid-shin down, were covered with blood.

Miraculously, he was alive and awake. He cried out in pain. Incredibly, from Allen's waist up little injury was incurred, just minor cuts and bruises — nothing that needed immediate attention. From the waist down, however, was a different story. The lower half of his body made the first impact with the hard asphalt, breaking bones in both legs and driving them through different parts of his flesh. Nothing from the waist down looked anatomically correct. At one compound fracture site, blood was flowing profusely. The bone, as well as the artery close to the bone, was ruptured. We needed to keep the fractured areas as immobile as possible while controlling the bleeding. Using utmost caution, I placed gauze on the fracture while applying pressure to stop the blood flow.

"This guy's taken his last step," I thought.

A large crowd was gathering. Not knowing any details, I assumed this guy had been working in the building and fell. The gentleman who called 911 stated that he was looking out his window from the building next door when he caught a glimpse of a person falling off the building.

I continued my assessment of his injuries and began to talk to him. "What happened, man?" I asked.

There was silence.

"What's your name?"

"Allen," he answered softly.

"Allen, how'd you fall, man?"

Again, there was silence.

"Allen, you need to talk to me, okay? You're badly hurt and I need you to stay awake and help us out with some information, okay?"

Allen said nothing.

We went on with anatomically realigning his legs the best we could and splinting them for transport. As the other guys placed him on a spine board, I headed to the truck to set up the IV's. On the way, a sheriff's officer gave me some interesting facts.

"I think this guy jumped," the officer said. "One of the tenants saw him walk to the balcony, climb over the railing, and jump. And if that's not enough, a bystander showed us the car he got out of. He had a gun and some shells in there, but the shells weren't the right ones for the gun. It looks like this guy is bent on doing himself in, but is sure having a rough time accomplishing it."

The officer's words confirmed the suspicions I'd had during Allen's silence. "I know this guy's hurting on the inside as much as on the outside," I thought to myself.

We loaded Allen into the truck. His vital signs were surprisingly stable, but I knew he needed the IV's in case things started going downhill.

I explained to him what I was doing. "Allen, I am starting these IV's to keep your blood pressure steady in case your legs or any possible internal injuries start to bleed. Okay? I don't want your body to go into shock. The IV's will help you. Your injuries are serious, Allen, and you are in need of a lot of medical attention. We are here to help you. Don't be afraid to talk to me. Okay?"

I could sense a feeling of trust in me on his part. I was also feeling the presence of the Holy Spirit guiding me to be sensitive to what the Lord would have me say during the twenty-minute ride to the hospital.

"Lord, you have your way," I prayed. With Allen properly packaged, I shut the back door.

"Let's go!" I yelled up front.

The siren rang out. Little did I know that this siren would become one more Siren For The Cross.

I bent down on one knee at Allen's side. "Allen, you can trust me, okay? I'm here to help you and I realize things must be pretty discouraging."

Allen took a deep breath. "I can't even kill myself right," he said reluctantly. Grimacing with pain, he made eye contact and said, "There's nothing worth living for."

I paused a moment before proceeding. "Allen, you know I think the Lord prevented you from taking your life today."

A puzzled "WHY?" look came across Allen's face.

"Yeah, Allen. The Lord watches over us sometimes when we

don't even realize it."

"Well, - - -" Allen responded, "I went to a Hindu gathering last week hoping to find some answers, but I got nothing." Looking away dejectedly he continued, "What's the use?"

God was opening a door of opportunity to share with this distressed individual. I took a deep breath. "Lord, give me the right words."

Pumping up the blood pressure cuff, I looked at Allen and said, "What you went to last week was a false attempt to know God. The only real knowledge of God and real purpose in your life is through Jesus Christ! You might not know Him, but I believe in my heart He stepped in and kept you from ending your life today. And you know what else? If you think things are bad now, they can't compare to the misery of how things would be if you'd died today not knowing the Lord."

Allen looked straight at me and asked a question I will never forget. "Do you mean if I had killed myself today I would have gone to hell?"

I responded, the only way I knew how. "Allen, the Bible says, 'He who has the Son has life and he who has not the Son has not life.' I'm glad you didn't die, Allen."

With pain on his face, he just stared into space. Silence hung around us. I could sense he was thinking God surely would have felt sorry for him if he had taken his life and would have taken him to heaven anyway. The verse I quoted hit Allen hard. Realizing this, I once again affirmed the fact that God had truly blocked him from taking his life and that He wanted to give Allen the purpose and meaning he so desperately sought in his life.

Despite his extensive pain, Allen appeared receptive to our conversation. His blood pressure was dropping, though. I opened up an IV. Allen remained awake and alert, a blessing in itself. I told him I needed to encode his condition to the hospital. We were about seven minutes out at this time.

The time I had left with Allen aboard the ambulance was

precious in more ways than one. I fully encoded the report in less than one minute. Returning to his side, I explained some of the things he could expect at the emergency room. While talking to him, Psalm 37:23-24 — "The steps of a man are established by the Lord" — came to mind and the Holy Spirit placed an overwhelming realization upon me: this was not a coincidence. It was by God's will that I was at Station 8 that day. He led me to Allen. Not only did this warm my heart, but I knew what God wanted me to say.

"Allen, you know I've been telling you all along that I know God intervened in your life. Well, I also know that God placed me in a position for our paths to cross. I wasn't supposed to be working today. All day I've wondered why I took this overtime. That was up until now! I know now why God arranged for me to be working in this response area. And I believe God also arranged for you to stop where you did. It was all in His perfect plan for you to know that He loves you and that He spared your life. God is using me to tell you. Can't you see that, Allen? God meant for me to be on duty to take care of you today!"

Allen still seemed dejected, but he listened to everything I said.

As I finished taking one more set of vitals, we pulled into the emergency entrance. Vitals were again stable. His mental and spiritual vitals were another story.

"Allen, we are at the hospital, okay. I'm sure once they stabilize you, they'll get you something for pain."

"I need it, man," Allen moaned.

"I know you do, and listen, Allen, I'm going to be praying for you."

Allen didn't say anything, but he did nod his head in approval.

Carefully, attempting to keep the numerous bone ends from grinding, we unloaded him. We wheeled him into the emergency room. The attending physician and nurses converged on him. I knew my private time with Allen was at an end.

"Get an orthopedic man up here stat!" I remember hearing as I headed toward the report room.

From then on, chaos ruled at his treatment area. Doctors and nurses ran back and forth tending to his needs. As I wrote my report, I wanted to share more about the Lord with Allen. "Maybe, somehow I'll get a chance to talk to him again," I thought.

I finished my report and went back to the treatment area. Allen's stall was empty.

"Where's Allen?" I asked, looking at the nurse's station.

"He's in X-ray," one of the nurses said.

I saw the emergency room physician who had examined Allen walking toward his desk, and figured I'd get his initial diagnosis.

"Do you think his lower legs can be saved?" I asked.

"Well, if he keeps them he will most likely never walk again," he said. "We'll just see what happens when the orthopedic surgeon gets hold of him."

I thanked him and walked back to the report room. The other guys had cleaned the truck and were ready to get back into service.

"I need to go to X-ray and see Allen before we go," I explained. "I'll be right back." I grabbed the hand-held radio and headed toward Allen. I knew things would be busy around him, but it really didn't matter. All I wanted to do was further convince him that I really cared and would be coming back to see him.

Allen was being moved from one X-ray area to another. He was heavily sedated from the pain medication. Still, he moaned softly under his breath.

"Allen, it's me, Tommy."

He opened his eyes and let out a soft, "Hey."

"Listen, Allen, I know things are going to be tough for a while. Just hang in there and remember I'm praying for you. I meant what I said in the truck. I've got to go now, but I'm going to be coming back to see you!"

Allen looked at me and softly said, "Okay, thank you." But I sensed he doubted I'd really come back.

As I headed back to the emergency room, I knew God had more work for me to do with Allen. I knew for sure I'd be seeing him again — hopefully at a quieter and less painful time.

We headed back to the station, talking about the uniqueness of this call. David would be relieving me in a couple of hours. I kept thinking, "I can't wait to tell David about this." I was irked at him earlier in the day for talking me into taking the overtime. I was now anxious to share God's wondrous ordering of all our steps.

Tommy Neiman and David French, partners and brothers in-the-Lord.

When David arrived, he listened attentively. He shared my awe and encouraged me to visit Allen.

The next day a close Christian brother, Steve Daffron, and I went to see Allen. I peeked into his room and noted massive numbers of bandages and splints on both legs.

"They saved them both," I happily thought.

Allen was groggy and appeared to be in great pain. "Hey, Allen," I said. "A lot of pain, huh?"

Allen cried out, "My legs are hurting so bad. I'm trying to rest but the pain is awful."

A nurse walked by. "Get me something for my pain! Now!" Allen yelled.

Then he looked at me. "And you — you can just leave me alone. I don't want to talk. Can't you see I'm in pain?"

"Okay," I responded. "I'll catch you later."

His eyes closed as he again cried out in pain.

I left the room. Six hours of surgery had taken its toll. This was not a good time to talk, and even though I felt like I had been delivered a spiritual blow, I knew God was working and I wasn't about to let Satan discourage me.

A couple of days passed before I paid Allen another visit. The pain had lessened and he was receptive. He realized my sincere offer to be his friend. Gradually he began to open up and share the dark secrets holding his heart in bondage. He related his family background and their strict Jewish beliefs. On a positive note, Allen told me about his godmother's son who forsook traditional Jewish belief and chose Christianity. This guy had even pursued a ministry in Christian music. In fact, he proudly told me, the man's group recently recorded its first album. But for the most part, Allen shared how meaningless life was and how frustration was consuming him.

I knew Allen needed hope. I knew he needed peace and meaning in life. I knew he needed a vision for the future, and I knew I needed God's guidance if I was to be used by Him.

I visited Allen repeatedly. Each visit, I shared new truths of God's great love. I reinforced each truth with an example from my life, where the love of Jesus Christ was evident.

All the while, God was preparing Allen's heart. It was during this time an elderly black lady was assigned to sit in Allen's room. I would see her quietly praying as I shared precious moments at Allen's bedside. That woman's quiet reassuring faith was, and always will be, an inspirational part of my life. I'm sure there were times when her faith made up for my doubts concerning Allen.

About two weeks after Allen's attempted suicide, a joyous moment took place in Allen's hospital room. Allen prayed with me to receive Jesus Christ as Lord and Savior. AMEN!

A week and a half later, another miracle occurred. Allen got out of bed and took several slow, but sure, steps.

Allen was also taking spiritual steps. He was studying the Bible and discussing the scriptures with me. Allen, now my brother-in-Christ, was becoming one of my closest friends.

A month later, Allen went home to Miami. He was not going alone, though. I was the one to take him to the hospital, and now I was honored and blessed to take him home from the hospital. My wife, Alicia, and three children were supportive in prayer and shared time as I visited and told Allen about God's love. On this special day, they accompanied me to pick Allen up and drive him to his sister's apartment, where he would live while continuing his therapy.

We drove to the front of the hospital. We waited for the nurses to bring Allen out in a wheel chair. But there was no wheel chair — no crutches — no walker — no cane. Allen walked out of that hospital with no support, and he walked out a new creature in Christ.

A little over a year from the date of the accident, I had the privilege of being the best man in his wedding.

Today, although hindered by occasional pain and a slight abnormality in his walk, Allen is being used by God in mighty ways through his involvement with a couple of Christian agencies that offer counseling services in the Miami area.

Allen knows without a doubt where he will spend eternity. He knows that his steps have been "established by the Lord," and he knows that the "Lord is the one who holds his hand."

A LIGHTER MOMENT

"There is an appointed time for everything . . ."

I Can't Tell You

A foreign refugee's makeshift raft split apart, leaving the occupant a captive of the ocean waters for two and one half days. A Coast Guard cutter picked him up and was bringing him in when they requested our assistance.

We met the cutter when it arrived at the Coast Guard station. Wasting no time, we carried the refugee off the ship and placed him on our stretcher. He was awake, dehydrated, and sunburned. His face reflected fear. No doubt he was overwhelmed by so many people in uniform. Before departing, the Coast Guard informed us that the refugee wasn't speaking at all, and consequently they were unable to get his name.

As we rolled the patient toward our rescue truck, I looked directly into his eyes and said, "No English?"

He nodded his head.

"Oh well," I thought, "I'll get him in the truck and then try to get him to tell me his name."

Once in the truck, we stacked blankets on him, gave him a little oxygen, and started toward the hospital. He appeared more relaxed. I knelt next to him and asked, "What is your name?"

"I'll can tell ya," came his mumbled reply.

"Ah, he does speak English," I thought. A little broken and blotched, but better than nothing.

I leaned over again and said, "But you can tell me, it's okay. What's your name?"

"I'll can tell ya. I'll can tell ya," came the frustrated reply.

This question and answer routine continued a little while longer before I finally gave up. I just motioned for him to rest, resigned to the probability of filling out a John Doe medical report.

The next day as I looked at the morning paper, there was a picture of us placing our sea drifter into the rescue truck. I didn't recall seeing cameras at the Coast Guard station but apparently there was at least one present, and obviously he got more information than I did, including one valuable piece — the man's name. The caption under the picture read, "Al Cantera is taken to a hospital after two and one half days in the ocean."

"Al Cantera," I said out loud. "So that's his name. The only thing I could get out of him was 'I'll can tell ya.'"

". . . A time to laugh."

ECCLESIASTES 3A: 1 AND 4B

CHAPTER 5

A Flash Of Light

"As he was traveling, it happened that he was approaching Damascus, and suddenly a light from heaven flashed around him; - - - and he (Paul) said who are You, Lord, and He said, 'I am Jesus . . .' "

ACTS 9:3-5

Early in my fire career, I was assigned to Station 11, one of the outlying stations in our county. This was a three-man station in which all of us were believers. Every third day, the three of us spent twenty-four consecutive hours together. We learned a lot about each other that people don't ordinarily learn on a regular eight-hour-per-day job. We became very close — like a family — a great second family. The lieutenant and station commander, Jeff Lightle, and I became exceptionally close — a friendship that continues to this day. Much of our down time was spent sharing scripture and talking about the Lord.

The sparsely populated area around this station covered a large section of the county and contained several two-lane roads with accelerated highway speed limits. There were not a lot of accidents on the seldom crowded roads. When one did occur, however, it was frequently horrendous — horrendous to the degree that whenever Station 11 was dispatched to an auto accident, other stations tuned in to our radio transmissions for information as to its seriousness. It was not unusual to witness death. But one Sunday afternoon, we witnessed life.

Billy, a twenty-one-year-old man, was driving toward our city from a nearby town. Alone in his mid-size car, he traveled one of those lone county roads in our station's response area.

Back at the fire station, we were enjoying a relaxed Sunday shift. We watched a couple of church service broadcasts on television, ate a big breakfast, napped, and headed out to play basketball behind the station.

"Ding!" The dispatch tones rang out on our station speakers. We halted our game before the basketball hit the pavement.

"Station 11, you have a signal four (an auto accident) two miles west of Header Canal Road, unable to advise further details," the dispatcher announced.

"It's way out there! This could be another bad one," I thought as I rushed toward the rescue truck.

We loaded up and headed west in the direction of the accident. As the ambulance lights flashed and the sirens wailed, we had no way of knowing that these sirens were destined to be literal Sirens For The Cross.

We said a prayer — a simple, but sincere prayer — asking God to be a part of everything that lay ahead. The answer was immediate — a quiet assuredness from the Holy Spirit at this anxious and nervous time.

As we continued toward the scene, I sought further details of the wreck from our dispatchers. The only information update available stated that Air One, our medical helicopter, was available and on standby if needed. We were thankful for that news, since the hospital was a lengthy distance from the scene of the accident. But I was surprised that law enforcement had not yet arrived. They are usually on the scene first and able to relay valuable information to us.

Twelve minutes after leaving the station we rolled up to

There were no police cars, no mangled cars, no trapped victims, and no life-threatening situations. There were heavy skid marks leaving the road in one direction.

the scene — an unusual scene at that. There were no police cars, no mangled cars, no trapped victims, and no life-threatening situations. There were heavy skid marks leaving the road in one direction. There was a very dirty, mud-encrusted car positioned 300 feet into an open field in the opposite direction from the skid marks.

While continuing to size up the scene, we assumed the driver of the car lost control and skidded off the road. But we were perplexed about how he ended up on the opposite side of the road so far off into the field.

From the length of the skid marks we deduced that the victim, Billy, was excessively exceeding the speed limit. He appeared unhurt. We notified central dispatch that we had a minor accident and they could take the helicopter off standby. We approached our victim.

"Are you all right?" I asked.

"Yeah, I guess so," he replied, shaking his head. A look of frustration — or was it disbelief — covered his face. "I just, uh, it's a long story," he continued.

"Come inside the rescue truck so we can check you out and make sure you're okay," I said.

He agreed. Jeff and I walked him to the truck and helped him inside. As he sat on the long bench seat that ran alongside the stretcher, I questioned him. "Are you hurting anywhere? Did you hit your head on anything?"

Looking down and without hesitation he replied, "No." Then he raised his head, looked at Jeff, and then turned to me and said, "Man, you're never going to believe what happened."

I looked at Jeff and I think we both knew at that moment

that God was working on this young man's heart. "It's okay," Jeff said in an assuring voice. "We'll understand."

Billy took a deep breath and began. "Well, for the past several days I think God has been trying to speak to me or something. I mean, I believe in God and all, but I'm just confused about who God really is. Anyway, I was driving over here to talk to some friends. The whole way over I was thinking about God and why I'm having such confusing thoughts. Suddenly, my car went out of control. I don't know how I lost it, but at the very moment I realized I was out of control, a bright flash of light surrounded me and a voice said, 'Hard to the right.' Without thinking about the light or the voice, I just closed my eyes and turned hard to the right. Next thing I knew I found myself sitting out in that field. Sounds crazy, huh?"

"No, not at all," Jeff replied.

"I believe that God was speaking to you," I added, remembering how Jesus appeared in a flash of light to Paul on his travels to Damascus. Paul was on his way to persecute believers in that far-off city when a bright light blinded him and Jesus said to him, "Paul, why are you persecuting me?" I was awed at the similarity. I was amazed at how God continues to speak in miraculous ways to this very day.

Billy looked downward. He shook his head in confusion. "Why is all this happening to me?" he said. "I just don't . . ."

"Billy, you could have gone into that canal and drowned," Jeff interrupted. "Your first skid marks off the road were directly in line with the canal, and that canal is deep with a long drop-off. I have no doubts that God sent that light, spoke to you, and kept you from death."

Billy slowly raised his head and said, "Yeah, I guess so."

I think Billy was beginning to realize there was a reason he was in the back of a rescue truck talking with two firefighters about God, and that he had no need for concern that Jeff and I would think him crazy. He relaxed, continued talking, and started making eye contact. We continued to reassure him of God's presence and how God led us to this call to assure him that it was God's voice in that "out of control" moment.

Jeff and I were certain God was at work preparing Billy's heart for salvation. Sensing God's prompting, I asked, "Billy, if you had gone into that canal and drowned or gone head-on and died when you crossed back over the road, do you know where you'd spend eternity?"

Billy hesitated, then said, "I don't know, but I hope I'd be in heaven."

Jeff spoke up. "Billy, the Bible says God loves us so much that He sent His only Son, that whoever believes in Him should not perish, but will certainly have — not might have — everlasting life."

Billy listened and turned toward me as I spoke. "And you know, Jesus wants to have a real and personal relationship with you, Billy. It's through this relationship that you are not only saved, but you can understand and trust God with everything that happens in your life."

Billy still seemed confused, but interested.

Jeff knew the moment was right. He seized the opportunity. "Billy, would you like to pray and ask Jesus to come into your heart and save you right now? Jesus promises us in the Bible that if we ask Him into our heart, He will come in."

Billy nodded his head in quiet agreement.

My heart sighed. I went over and put my arm on Billy's shoulder as Jeff led him through a believer's prayer of salvation. Praise God!

A smile erupted on Billy's face when we finished praying. He was a new creation — a child of God. Jeff and I were on cloud nine. We shared more about his new walk, about reading the Bible, and about praying.

As Billy exited the back door of the rescue truck, the first highway patrolman was just arriving. "Hum!" I wondered. "Who kept him away so long!"

I'll bet that patrolman wondered why this accident victim was smiling when he stepped out of the rescue truck. There was no way he could know that instead of death, Billy now had Life — Eternal Life in Jesus Christ.

A LIGHTER MOMENT

"There is an appointed time for everything . . ."

Smilin' Mighty Jesus

Not too long after I started on the fire department, I was sent to a new station in the South End. When I opened my duffel bag, Steve noted my Bible on top of some clothes. This sparked an interesting conversation. We first talked about our respective churches. Then he said, "Hey, I've got a call you'll really appreciate."

I responded, "Oh ya, tell me."

He immediately began his story.

About a month ago Steve had received a 'weakness' call. He arrived to find an older gentleman who seemed quite illiterate and definitely hard of hearing. He walked up to the man and said, "Sir, what's going on today?"

"I got the smilin' mighty Jesus," the man responded.

"Excuse me. Could you repeat that?" Steve asked, speaking a little louder.

"I got the smilin' mighty Jesus."

Realizing he might not be hearing him clearly, he moved a little closer to him.

"Could you repeat that v-e-r-y s-l-o-w-l-y?"

"I . . . .got . . . . the . . . . smilin' . . . . mighty . . . Jesus," came the drawn-out reply.

Steve thought, "Oh well. I guess we'll never figure this one out." Then a bright idea came over him. "Do you have any papers from your doctor?"

The guy pointed to the table. Sure enough, he had medical papers from his home health nurse, the contents of which made him quiver and regret his close proximity.

This man might very well have had the "smilin' mighty Jesus," for he appeared to be a man of faith, but the medical papers didn't say that. No, the papers didn't refer to his condition as "smilin' mighty Jesus" — but a very contagious form of spinal meningitis!

". . . A time to laugh."

ECCLESIASTES 3A: 1 AND 4B

CHAPTER 6

The Night Of The Church Fire

"And He (God) put all things in subjection under His (Christ's) feet and gave Him head over all things to the church which is His body, the fullness of Him who fills all in all."

EPHESIANS 1:22-23

Shortly after promotion to engineer/driver, I was transferred to Central Fire Station, a station noted for its abundance of fire calls. I was nervous and anxious over the opportunity to drive and operate one of the new fire engines our department had recently purchased. I eagerly anticipated the excitement of stomping down on the gas pedal with sirens screaming and air horns blaring, while tunneling through busy traffic to the sight of heavy black smoke ahead. And, to have this opportunity on nearly every shift was overwhelming. On the practical side, I realized the activity would provide a valuable opportunity for gaining the fire experience a new engineer needed.

While the action at Central was steady and invigorating, it seemed as though the "Big One" was alluding us. I didn't wish disaster on anyone, but the firefighter inside me longed for more action. I began to wonder when, and if, we would get a big-time structure fire.

Then it happened, and today this fire still stands out as the most memorable highlight of my time spent as an engineer at Central Fire Station. Not just because it was a large fire, but because the Lord's peace and His ever-assuring presence were exceptionally real to me that night. I call it, "The Night of the Church Fire."

There was little action during the day. We were drifting into a quiet evening as well until, about 8:00 p.m., a call came in. Two sets of alarm tones sounded. Our adrenaline level soared as we realized two stations' entire companies were responding. "This must be a good working fire," I thought. Immediately we sprang into action. As an engineer, I headed for the driver's seat of Engine 1 as the crew bunkered out in fireproof boots, suspendered fire pants, bunker coats, hoods, and helmets. The winds howled outside as we pulled out of the fire station. Whiffs of smoke reached our nostrils.

Engine 1 was the first to leave the station. We were the station closest to the fire and would be the first-in pumper. My heart was beating through my chest as our sirens screamed through traffic. As I manuevered the truck through busy streets, the crew put on their self-contained breathing apparatus and gloves. I sensed their excitement and readiness as they spurred me on. "Go Tommy, go!"

"We finally got a big one," I yelled, jamming the pedal as hard as I could to the floor.

Three intersections ahead we saw heavy smoke concealing the traffic lights. No doubt, we had a working fire! The first big challenge was to get through that intersection of heavy smoke, traffic, and spectators to the burning structure just beyond. The smoke intensified as we pulled up to the intersection. Visibility was nearly zero. I slowed the engine and crept into a right turn, all the while praying, "Lord, don't let me hit anything!" We advanced past the wind-pushed smoke, allowing me to get a good look at the involved structure — a large, wooden, country-style church. But not just any church, as you'll eventually see.

Smoke poured out of the large sanctuary windows. Hidden

almost entirely by the smoke was a drive-through hamburger restaurant just a few feet away. I continued to size up the scene. The restaurant was open and operating. That meant the possibility of people being near the dangerous burning structure. Fortunately, a fire hydrant was on the next block, only yards away from the church. We quickly drove to it, hung a U-turn, and dropped off a large hose line from our supply bed. As soon as it was wrapped around the hydrant, I headed for the fire.

The commanding officer called out directions. "Tommy, move that supply line."

I complied.

Next, I positioned the truck on the busy crowded street right between the burning church and the hamburger restaurant. As the guys jumped off the truck, a major intensification of the fire took place. The heavy smoke pouring out of the sanctuary windows was replaced by leaping flames — flames that were licking up against and beginning to melt the restaurant's exterior plastic lighting fixtures.

The incident command officer called out, "Evacuate the restaurant." Aided by law enforcement, more than twenty restaurant patrons were quickly scampering across the street to safer ground.

Our guys immediately grabbed the hose lines and disappeared into the clouds of thick, black smoke between the church and the restaurant. I yanked the gate valves and pumped as much water through their hose lines and nozzles as they could handle.

The fire flared. My mind buzzed. "Can we save the restaurant from going down with the church? Can our guys fight back the torch-like flames from those sanctuary windows?"

I prayed for them as I stood at the truck's pump panel. They were only fifty feet away from me, yet they were completely hidden in the flames and smoke.

We were forced into a defensive mode. Obviously the church faced total destruction. We needed to contain the fire. Our new objective was to keep it from consuming the surrounding structures.

More engines and fire trucks arrived. We initiated the procedures for gaining control of a major fire. It was a slow process. The minutes dragged on. For a solid hour and a half we relentlessly tackled the flames. Another half hour passed. Progress, at last. The hamburger restaurant was saved from internal damage. But the church fire, while contained, continued to burn for several more hours.

During the efforts of controlling this fire, a flood of thoughts swept over me. As I stood at my pump panel controlling the flow of water, I felt as if Satan were on the war path in my mind. He seemed to be mocking the church, taunting me with his deception, and calling out to me, "See how I am destroying your Lord's house with fire!" I even felt as if I heard his evil chuckles in the crackles of the flames.

I shook off those thoughts. I focused on the Lord, and as I did the Lord reminded me that a building is not the church. The church is the people, God's people, people who are indwelled with "the fullness of Him who fills all in all."

I was fighting a battle of my own. During the long hours, as the flames continued to destroy the magnificent country-style church, I was overcome with sadness.

As a part of the church, the precious body of Christ, I counted my blessings. I praised God that nothing can destroy the real church.

I was fighting a battle of my own. During the long hours, as the flames continued to destroy the magnificent country-style church, I was overcome with sadness. Despite my efforts to stay focused on Christ, I felt as if Satan were prevailing and chalking this up as his victory.

Silly thoughts passed through my mind — thoughts that could only come from the evil one. "The people that were saved in this church aren't saved anymore because the church is being lost to fire," Satan seemed to say.

"Don't even try that one, you scumbag," was my immediate thought in response. "Every single solitary decision for Jesus that took place in that building is as much alive today as the day it happened. And furthermore, Satan, you can't even look at the hand that's holding those precious souls, let alone even think about snatching them out of God's hand."

A real peace and thankfulness began to flow over me as the exact words of God's promise came to mind: ". . . and I give eternal life to them, and they will never perish; and no one will snatch them out of My hand." (John 10:28).

While I was effortlessly monitoring that control panel, the Lord flooded my heart with memories. I remembered visiting this church long ago with friends. As a young boy, I remembered looking into the choir loft and imagining how neat it would be to sit up there. I recalled visiting years later when my younger brother, Terry, an associate pastor there at the time, preached God's word. It was his first sermon. I sat with my family. None of us wanted to miss this momentous occasion.

Now in the midst of the destruction before me, God's peace calmed and comforted me as I refocused on His wonders. I knew beyond a doubt that He was still in control.

Satan lost his power to shoot any more fiery darts that night. I am sure that if Satan tried to continue his assault, God reminded him of the burning fire and the lake where he is doomed to spend eternity.

Oh yeah, as for the building — it was totally destroyed, but the body of believers that make up that church has greatly increased in their new church building.

A building is not the church. The church is the people, God's people.

Photo compliments of Jack White, Indianapolis Fire Department.

A LIGHTER MOMENT

"There is an appointed time for everything . . ."

What's That Chirp

Stories of real-life incidents often help us pass time when calls are slow at the station. Recently, a fireman relayed an incident that still causes me to chuckle.

At 3:00 a.m. a lady called his station. "My pacemaker is malfunctioning," she complained.

The guys on shift responded. When they arrived they found an elderly lady living alone. She appeared all right physically. Emotionally she was distraught.

In the stillness of the night, upon entering the house, the rescue crew heard a sudden "chirp" sound. Ignoring it, they crossed the room to the little old lady who was sitting anxiously on the couch.

"What's wrong, ma'am?" one of the guys said.

"It's my pacemaker. I think there is something wrong with it. It keeps going off."

The guys were somewhat bewildered as they hooked her up to the EKG monitor and all looked fine. Just then they heard the chirp-like sound again.

"There it goes again," the lady cried out. "Every little while it goes off like that! I just know my pacemaker is acting up and I need to get it fixed."

The guys looked up. Immediately they suspected where the noise came from. They felt certain it was the smoke detector on the wall that was making the occasional sound to tell her the batteries needed to be changed. They waited a moment to confirm their suspicions. Again, the chirp sounded.

"See," the lady said, "it keeps doing that!" The guys looked at each other and discreetly shook there heads. From that point on the biggest challenge was keeping a straight face while explaining "that chirp" to the lady.

". . . A time to laugh."

ECCLESIASTES 3A: 1 AND 4B

CHAPTER 7

A Seízure?

"The thief comes only to steal and kill and destroy; I came that they may have life, and have it abundantly."

JOHN 10:10

If there is anything I have grown to hate as a rescue worker, it's seeing drugs and alcohol directly or indirectly destroy people. These are no less than the tools Satan uses in his efforts — as recorded in scripture — to steal, kill, and destroy (John 10:10).

Alcohol abuse calls are so plentiful I could spend hours recounting horrific accidents and needless tragedies. But for this chapter, I would like to relate two calls that depict Satan's sting behind the use of drugs. In particular, the use of a drug we have heard about all too frequently.

The first call was a response to a residence where a person was supposedly having seizures. We arrived on scene to find a sixteen-year-old girl lying on a couch shaking viciously. The house was filled with teenagers and loud music. Empty beer cans littered the premises and the odor of marijuana filled the air. The girl in distress obviously wasn't hindering the large amount of partying going on. Perhaps most of the partygoers thought she was just riding a good drug trip. Fortunately, the girl's best friend was with her and knew this wasn't the girl's typical behavior. Intelligently, she located a phone and called "911."

Shortly after our arrival, the police department arrived on

> **The girl continued to shake violently. She kept yelling hysterically in chopped-up words, "I'm burning up, I'm burning up."**

scene and things began to settle down. Someone turned the music off as others began to converge on the room we were in.

The girl continued to shake violently, but she was awake and was pulling wildly at her clothes, her face, her hair — at anything she could grab in the midst of her extreme behavior. She kept yelling hysterically in chopped-up words, "I'm burning up, I'm burning up."

This was certainly unlike any seizure I'd ever witnessed before, and I've been on lots of seizure calls. Besides, in severe or grand mal seizures, the patient is usually unresponsive. This girl was awake and trying to make short, rapid attempts at talking. Her shaking and violent movements increased, making it impossible for her to form complete sentences. Her face and jaw muscles trembled, further hindering her attempts at speech. I had serious suspicions that this was not a seizure. I tried to take her blood pressure. It was a futile attempt, for the muscles in her arms were full of spasms. Frustrated, I yelled out, "Does anyone know if this girl has a history of seizures?"

Finally her best friend — breaking into tears — blurted out one of my suspicions. "She tried some crack for the first time a few minutes ago."

"Thank you," I responded point blank.

I had heard about first-time reactions to cocaine, but hadn't yet encountered one. After seeing this girl I could see why death can happen after one try of this Satan-laced drug, and I thought perhaps this just might be one of those cases — especially after seeing her heartbeat on my cardiac monitor. It was almost 300! Incredible!

Never had I witnessed a heart rate that fast. I thought her heart was literally going to explode or that a vessel or valve would rip and her heart would just quit. The rapid flutter over the chest wall covering her heart was frightfully visible. Sweat ran off her head and body in torrents. Every part of her body seemed to be reacting in its own violent manner. Her head jerked from side to side, slamming each side of her face on the couch where she lay. Her hands, which were grabbing at anything and everything, began raking and clawing at the area over her heart. Even her toes clenched and extended angrily out of control.

The erratic and uncontrolled behavior of the girl, coupled by the rapid beeps of my monitor recording her heartbeat, made the majority of onlookers aware of the magnitude of her condition. A silence filled the house. But even in the midst of the surrounding stillness, trying to get this girl to calm down was like walking through a brick wall.

I grasped the moment of silence, hoping all would hear my comment as I quickly, but very loudly, said to my guys, "I can see how people might die from using crack; we need to get her to the hospital fast!"

Hopefully a penetrating message was left behind. We loaded the girl into the ambulance and I quickly called the emergency room to tell them what we had.

"I have some heart-slowing medications on board if needed," I advised the emergency room doctor.

He advised of their ineffectiveness and said, "Just rapid transport!"

An IV was out of the question due to her uncontrollable shaking. We oxygenated her the best we could and delivered her in rapid fashion to the ER.

With airway support, oxygen therapy, and eventual IV fluids, the girl lived. We later learned it took several hours for her heart rate to come down from the fatal range it was in. The Lord just protected her heart. Period.

She should have been a statistic. I don't know how much she remembers, as it was impossible to communicate with her in that uncontrollable state, but I do know there were many young people witnessing a potential death in the making. Maybe a good motto for crack cocaine should be, "One try . . . and you just might die."

I'm convinced from seeing the suffering and violence that crack cocaine produces that the only thing it does is make the voice of Satan ring loud in your ears. Such was the case with a twenty-five-year-old man we responded to one morning. He called from a pay phone, stating he was sick and living on the street. We found him in an area behind an old abandoned building, sitting on what was left of the building's air conditioning unit. He was dirty, unkempt, roughed up, and crying. Yes . . . crying. When I confronted him, he reached out and took hold of my hand. "I need help, man. I can't go through what I did last night and this morning."

He went on to share how he tried cocaine for the first time the night before. He stated he had been on the streets for the last two weeks, but had never before touched drugs. In fact, he said he was planning to go back home and start over.

"But this morning," he continued, "something told me I had to have more of the stuff I tried last night. I saw a lady walking on the street and that same voice told me to take that lady's purse so I could get some more of that stuff. The voice kept yelling at me to go — go take it now."

He placed his head in his hands and said, "I just freaked — I can't live like this."

I clutched hold of his hand and shared with him how the Lord kept him from assaulting that woman. I further told him that the voice he heard was straight from the mouth of Satan himself.

"But it was so real and loud in my ear."

"Listen, man," I responded. "That drug makes Satan's voice come alive in your mind, and I have no doubt that you actually heard it. But the awesome power of God is far greater than anything Satan can say or do."

I looked him hard in the eye. "Are you a believer, man?" I asked.

"Yeah, but I've lived far apart from Him," he stated.

"That's doesn't mean He's lived far apart from you," I responded. I could tell this guy was really starting to sense and appreciate what God was doing. I felt the Lord's presence surrounding and loving this man.

He continued to weep.

I put my hand on his shoulder, "I really feel like God arranged for me to be with you here today, brother."

He looked at me and nodded in agreement. I'm sure he realized at that moment that more than "911" was responding to his call for help.

I explained how I could get him continued help through a health facility if he would consent to go. He graciously agreed. I further told him about the help he would be receiving, but left it clear that the greatest help was already on the inside of his heart.

A policeman came to initiate the treatment process. As they walked away, I got the man's attention one more time. "Hey, man … I'm praying for ya!"

Three days later he completed his treatment and returned home.

As I look back on these two calls, it is unmistakably evident that Satan is out to destroy both the body and the mind through this drug we call crack cocaine. The only hope of victory for the body and the mind is Christ in the heart. The only hope of completely defeating Satan's attempt to defeat a person with this mind-deceiving, flesh-devouring, addictive drug is through Christ.

Regardless of the sin or temptation in your life, with Christ in your heart, you have the very power of God to make you victorious over Satan.

Have you tried Jesus?

The Bible tells us, ". . . greater is He (Jesus) that is in us, than he that is in the world" (1 John 4:4). It also says that Christ came so that you "may have life, and have it abundantly" (John 10:10).

And that's a promise!

A LIGHTER MOMENT

"There is an appointed time for everything . . ."

Johnny's Going Nowhere

Combine a five-year-old boy, a chair, and a cool, calm, and collected mother and you have the makings of an amusing call.

The tones rang. The dispatcher called out, "a child stuck in a chair."

We arrived at the child's home to find the child, little Johnny, with his head wedged through two of the rails on the backrest of a dining room chair. He wasn't crying, and his mom didn't seem unusually upset. In fact, from the time we entered the house until we left, the mom merely related one incident after another about how Johnny ran around and got into everything.

Johnny finally met his match when he started playing with that dining room chair. And now, there he was, bending over with his head sticking out of the two rails and his hands grasping onto the other rails of the backrest. He was going nowhere. Little Johnny, looking as if he were a prisoner behind jail bars, just held onto the other rails with a look of puzzlement as if to say, "Are you going to free me from this cell?"

Meanwhile, his mother looked at us and said, "Wow,

you-all were fast getting here. Maybe you should wait awhile. I don't know if you should get him out just yet!"

Johnny, held captive as she spelled out the reports of his behavior, looked from us to his mother as if wondering if his mom would allow us to free him from the chair.

When she halted her friendly discourse, we coated the sides of his head with K-Y Jelly, pulled on the rails, and rather easily freed Johnny from his temporary prison.

Without a word, he immediately left us and went to play with his brothers and sisters in the front yard.

As we walked out to the truck, his mother yelled, "Do you think he might do that again?"

Wishful thinking, mom!

". . . A time to laugh."

ECCLESIASTES 3A: 1 AND 4B

CHAPTER 8

Passing Sunrise

". . . to be absent from the body and to be at home with the Lord."

2 CORINTHIANS 5:8

The advancement in the field of emergency medical service amazes me. As paramedics, we continually perform more medical treatment — treatment that was previously done only in the emergency room. Likewise, our equipment is more sophisticated and technical. Areas of increased involvement with improved equipment include pacing hearts, monitoring blood oxygenation levels, assessing twelve-lead EKG readings, administering "clot busters" in the midst of heart attacks, and administering numerous other medications in various life-and-death situations. It's not uncommon for a rescue crew to walk into a house armed with over $15,000 worth of medical equipment — all with the goal of saving life.

Yet, with all this equipment, technology, and training, we are sometimes forced to acknowledge that "life at all cost and effort" takes a back seat to God's perfect timing in calling someone home. This truth was made clear one early Sunday morning.

The call came in at about 5:30 in the morning: "An unresponsive person."

"An unresponsive person" is potentially, as well as frequently, a code situation where the patient has no heart beat and is not breathing. Our job is to try to revive the patient by getting the heart pumping, initiating CPR, delivering 100% oxygen, and performing any other life-saving measures the particular situation merits — all in an attempt to save a life.

We responded with a rescue engine and full complement of manpower. It was a quiet neighborhood. Our very presence seemed to violate the peacefulness of the calm morning air. Our destination was a little wooden house with a quaint warm countenance. The three of us on the rescue truck each grabbed two items of medical equipment and rushed toward the house. As we scurried across the dewy grass, I noticed how the fire engine's outside radio speakers interrupted the stillness of this serene neighborhood. A young lady met us at the door. "My aunt isn't responding."

"Where is she?"

"Down the hallway, last door to the right," she answered in a shaky voice.

The house was dimly lit. The only light was the beacon light of our truck flashing against the walls of her living room. We hurried down the short, dark hallway, our radios buzzing with static. The heavy equipment bumped against the walls. We created the general appearance of massive chaos in this otherwise peaceful home atmosphere. I was the first one in the tiny room. It, too, was dark. The only light came from the nearness of daybreak in the lady's bedroom windows. I took a few unsuccessful swipes on the doorway-area walls in hope of finding a light switch. I found none.

"Find a light," I stated to the guys behind me as I went to the woman's bedside to get an assessment.

The guys unloaded their equipment at their feet. This alone literally shook the feeble wooden floor underneath us. As one of them headed for a small lamp on the dresser, I reached out and touched the woman's wrist.

"Never mind that light," I said. "We aren't gonna be working her. She's gone."

She was quite cool, indicating she had passed some time

ago. There was no need to even confirm with an EKG.

"Go ahead and take our stuff back to the truck," I told the guys. "And shut the flashers down, okay?"

The guys left, again lugging the heavy medical equipment through the now solemn house. Their footsteps once again echoed loudly on the old wooden floor.

I met the niece in the living room. "I'm afraid we were not in time!" I said with compassion.

Sobbing quietly, she said, "My aunt was ill for sometime. And, . . ." she paused, "she was a woman of great faith."

I nodded my head. I shared with her the peace her aunt was now experiencing. Next I explained that a law enforcement officer would come to take a report and that we would stay with her until he arrived. After encouraging her to sit down, I left to gather the remaining equipment in her aunt's room.

> *The room had taken on a whole new perspective. It appeared that a light switch had been turned on.*

I virtually tiptoed back down that narrow hallway. As I quietly edged my way into the bedroom, I was stunned. The room had taken on a whole new perspective. It appeared that a light switch had been turned on. Daybreak illuminated the room as if to purposely highlight the decor of this recently departed soul's bedroom.

The niece's words, "a woman of great faith" rang out in my mind as I looked about the room and saw abundant evidence of a Lord and Savior she loved. Her wall was littered with plaques exclaiming great verses of the Bible. Each dresser and table in her room was decorated with crosses and wooden artwork that said "Jesus" on them. Her night stand, only inches away from where her head lay resting, yielded an old, rugged, large-print Bible. It was opened to the twenty-third Psalm. The Holy Spirit overwhelmed me as I touched that old tattered and torn Word of God. "God surely gave her insight to this Psalm on this her final reading of the Bible," I thought.

I stood in awe beside her bed as the spiritual peacefulness of the moment consumed me. And then it dawned on me: we came with an abundance of modern technical equipment, these flashing lights and sirens, all in the name of saving physical life — and in many cases this is well warranted. But there are times — such as the spiritual beauty of this one — where all this human effort, all these human accessories, are but a mockery to the wonderful unfolding of a loving Father calling a precious child home.

If this lady could have spoken, I'm sure she would have said, "Don't even think about bringing me back." The apostle Paul said, ". . .to be absent from the body (is) to be at home with the Lord" — just like that! No waiting! An instantly fulfilled promise of God! At this very moment, she was on heaven's shore experiencing life in a way we can only speculate and dream of.

Her departure made a deep impression on this young and aggressive paramedic. How totally awesome it must be when Jesus comes to take you by the hand to leave your earthly body. The joy must be incomparable, the love overwhelming, and the peace beyond description.

My spirit was ministered to in the early hours of this peaceful morning. And, as I picked up the equipment and headed toward the door, I noticed the room suddenly brighten. I turned to see the sunrise give way to the first rays of the morning sun as they came streaming through her bedroom window. The rays shone across her night stand, across the Bible, and onto this woman's face which revealed an ever-so-slight smile. She had seen Jesus coming for her. And today she was "absent from the body" and "home with the Lord."

CHAPTER 9

You Better Pray That Prayer

"Trust in Lord with all your heart and do not lean on your own understanding. In all your ways acknowledge Him and He will make your paths straight."

PROVERBS 3:5

It was a Friday night. I was on duty at Fire Station 4, one of the busier stations in our county. The shift, which began at 7:30 that morning, was unusually slow for most of the day. We'd been canceled on a fire alarm and had answered one minor medical call. Other than that, our station tones had been silent.

"Could we actually have an easy shift on a Friday?" I thought to myself.

I quickly dismissed that thought and concluded we were being saved until after midnight. I figured I'd at least throw a piece of chicken on the grill while things were quiet.

That chicken never made it to the grill. Instead, the tones sounded and we were dispatched to a "shooting!"

My rampant imagination went into gear as it does every time a call for a shooting comes in. Little information was available from the initial call. I hurried toward the rescue truck, my mind exploring the many possibilities. How many people were hit? Where were they shot? How many entrance wounds? Exit wounds? Are there still bullets flying around at the scene? With a scarcity of information available, I simply expected anything and everything.

Making our way through traffic, I put on my latex gloves, making sure they were as high up on my arms as possible. Shootings always meant blood and sometimes lots of it. I assumed this would be no exception.

Turning into the neighborhood, I observed a large gathering one block ahead. There were already four or five police units around the scene, which was comforting. As we eased through the crowd and pulled up close to the scene, we got our first glimpse of the victim, a young man lying in a pool of blood in the middle of the road. I grabbed my trauma bag and headed to his side.

Upon initial examination, I noticed he had at least two bullet holes. One was in his shoulder; the other looked like it entered through his upper arm and traveled into his side. I assessed his level of consciousness. It was rapidly decreasing. He struggled to stay awake, opening his eyes only momentarily to loud verbal stimuli. He was going downhill fast. We needed to move quickly. My partner and I pressure-bandaged the bleeding bullet holes and placed him in a military anti-shock suit, a garment designed to improve his blood pressure and oxygenate his vital organs.

We continued to work. The crowd pressed in around us., and we needed room to get the patient on a backboard. I surveyed our surroundings. One desperate look at a nearby police officer remedied the situation. He quickly cleared the immediate area. We strapped our victim onto the backboard and lifted him onto the stretcher.

This guy was in critical condition. He was no longer opening his eyes. Treatment was imperative. I felt relieved that we were near the rescue truck and would soon be away from this crowded scene. Then the most unusual thing occurred. As we wheeled the stretcher toward the door, a lady came out of the crowd. She began walking alongside the head end of the stretcher. I presumed her to be a family member, as she began firmly calling this man's name.

Knowing there were only seconds before we would have him in the truck, she yelled in his face some words I will never forget. "Listen, man, you remember that prayer I told you to pray? You'd better pray it!"

We began to load the stretcher.

She yelled at him again, "That prayer I told you about, you'd better pray it!"

We closed the back doors. She was sobbing. Confusion covered her face as if she were wondering, "Did he even hear me in his state of unconsciousness?"

This paramedic did hear her, though, and I couldn't help but wonder what sort of prayer she was talking about. Even in the midst of transport, as I continued to push IV fluids in hopes of keeping this guy alive, her challenge to him kept surfacing in my mind. I wondered, "Could that prayer she was referring to be a prayer of salvation or was it some ritualistic group of words with some sort of magical power that would heal him? Or was it perhaps a cultic chant that she falsely believed would save his soul if he died?"

The sirens blared on. The lights flashed and my mind raced on. We reached the hospital and successfully transferred this guy to the emergency room staff in a more stable condition than we found him. Hopefully, he would make it.

As I lay in my bunk that night, the woman's words about that mysterious prayer plagued my mind. I came to the conclusion that this prayer could very well have been a prayer of salvation and her concern was that his lost soul was about to go into a Christless eternity. At first, I thought this was good. But the more I considered it as a prayer for salvation, the more judgmental I became. Bitterness crossed my mind. Who does this guy think he is? Does he think he can live the way he wants and then call on God at the last moment for a bailout!

My mind sped on. Living the life he wanted probably got

him shot, anyway. After all, this was drug related. And now that he's dying, she's reminding him not to forget to get saved. Sort of like "get into trouble and maybe die, then call upon God!"

Who would ever do something like that? Certainly not me, right?

Wrong!

A few months after that incident, I was called out on a structure fire. A small, confined warehouse littered with old appliances and furniture was engulfed with dark smoldering clouds of

Backdraft Explosions are extremely dangerous.
Miraculously a fellow firefighter was not injured in this explosion.

Photo courtesy of the Fort Pierce Tribune, Florida

smoke. It was into this inferno of suffocating smoke that my lieutenant and I crawled in search of the seat of the fire, in search of that faint glow in the dark, bleak, smoke-filled building. As I was hanging onto the hose line for dear life, I began to feel parts of the roof land on the back of my air pack and helmet. The warehouse had only two doors. There was an imminent danger of a backdraft causing a life-ending explosion. The smoke was tremendous. The danger of suffocation was great, and the possibility of burning to death wasn't far-fetched, especially if I were trapped by a falling roof.

"I'm going to die in here," I feared. "I really am."

I began dealing with God. "Lord, if You'll just get me out of here, I'll serve You better. Lord, I'll teach Sunday School and I'll help with the youth, just don't let me die in this building!"

The Lord wasn't ready to take me home that day. We managed to get out of that building alive, escaping by crawling our way back out along that precious hoseline before the structure was totally consumed. But it wasn't long after catching my breath that I realized I was no different from the man and woman at the shooting incident. I, too, was dealing with God in the face of trouble.

The man survived his shooting and I survived that burning inferno. I wondered if he ever prayed that prayer. I may never know, but I do know that I thank God for His great forgiveness, His awesome mercy, and His unfathomable love — all through His Son, Jesus Christ. I know God would rather not have us make deals. He also doesn't want us judging others as I was wrongfully doing. But His desire is for us to obey Him at all times, trust Him with all our heart, and not rely on our own understanding. (Proverbs 3:5). We should especially never wait to acknowledge Christ as Savior and Lord, for we never know when a shot will be fatal.

A LIGHTER MOMENT

"There is an appointed time for everything . . ."

Anything His Little Heart Desires

Joey was six years old. He was on an adventure at the beach, across the street from the fire station where I was the paramedic on duty. While happily playing in the surf, he came in contact with a man-o-war. These jellyfish-like creatures have long, invisible tentacles with little stingers that inflict pain when they come into contact with the skin.

Joey was feeling pain. He was screaming. His mom grabbed the crying child, rushed across the street, and placed her howling child on our kitchen table. Together, mom and paramedic started the tedious task of calming the youngster down. All the while, I explained to mom that the red marks were most likely man-o-war stings and, since Joey wasn't having any signs of a full-body reaction, he would be okay.

Joey obviously disagreed and wanted everyone in the fire station to know he was hurting.

It was lunch time and the other firemen were preparing their lunch in the kitchen. They all wished Joey had a volume control knob.

One of the guys tried the "here's a cookie if you stop crying" trick.

It worked! Little Joey actually paused a moment as he took the cookie and held it.

"We're getting somewhere," I thought.

The warm ammonia and water solution I was gently swabbing on his sting marks was probably alleviating some of the pain as well.

Joey sniffed and let out an occasional cry. He looked around. He noticed one of the other guys fixing two hot dogs down the counter from him.

"I like hot dogs," whimpered Joey.

Sure enough, within a minute, Joey had a half-eaten cookie in one hand and a hot dog in the other. His pain appeared to be decreasing rapidly.

"You're being so brave today," I responded. "I'll bet you were having all kinds of fun until that mean jellyfish stung you!"

Joey nodded as he bit into his hot dog. Seeing one of the guys turn on the television in the adjoining day room, I told Joey about us having a television just like he did at home. Thinking about my little five year old at home, I said, "I'll bet you like Nickelodeon."

"Uh, hum," Joey said. "I watch it all the time." Then came the clincher. "Could you put it on Nickelodeon?" Joey confidently asked pointing to the television.

I looked up at the guy who had not only lost a hot dog but was going to miss his midday sports report. "Sure," I laughingly said, motioning for that "slightly angered but not showing it" firefighter to turn the channel to Nickelodeon.

At this point we knew our fire station had been taken over by a five year old. Fortunately, Joey's mom also realized this and told Joey that since his "boo-boo" was better, it was time to go and tell all the nice firemen good-bye.

Just then, Joey's wounds began to hurt again. So much so that he told me I needed to start swabbing the cloth on his leg some more. I watched Joey as he quickly turned his focus back to the television program. I looked at his mom. She smiled as she lifted the little boy from the table.

"Joey, listen honey. We need to go. You are all better now and this isn't our house, although I know you think it is," she said, smiling at us.

Just then someone opened the freezer. And something inside caught little Joey's eye. I guess Joey's mom wasn't walking fast enough toward the front door, because little Joey had a bowl of ice cream before he left.

". . . A time to laugh."

ECCLESIASTES 3A: 1 AND 4B

CHAPTER 10

A Call For Spiritual Warfare

"For our struggle is not against flesh and blood, but against the rulers, against the powers, against the world forces of this darkness, against forces of wickedness in the heavenly places."

EPHESIANS 6:12

In Ephesians 6:12 the Apostle Paul addresses spiritual warfare in high places. He speaks of wrestling against rulers of the darkness in this world. Throughout my Christian life, I've heard this passage numerous times. I realized supernatural battles occur and are presently in progress in the spiritual world. I have given thought to the potential that battles in the spiritual realm might break through in supernatural ways in our everyday lives. However, I never really contemplated the great extent to which Paul was cautioning believers until a few years ago, when I answered a very unusual rescue call.

The call was dispatched as a "sick person" call. It came in on an ordinary weekday morning. We were busy with our usual morning duties and even though this call didn't sound exciting, I was glad for a break from washing fire trucks.

The address was a convenience store on one of the main roads in our city. The store had a pay phone on the outside wall. We figured our "sick person" probably made the call.

Our suspicions were confirmed as we pulled onto the scene and saw an older man crouched near the phone. He was heavily clothed for a warm summer morning. His tattered and torn tennis shoes and plastic bag of odds and ends indicated he was a vagrant street person. The musty smell of moldy clothes, mingled with the smell of stale alcohol on both his clothes and breath, was overpowered only by the odor of perspiration from too many unlaundered clothes on one person for such a warm summer day. His fatigued eyes reflected both frustration and anger.

I have tended many vagrants throughout my career and have become accustomed to the bitterness projected by many. However, experience has taught me that most want only a good meal and a place to sleep before returning to life on the streets. I assumed this case would be no exception. We'd just check him out, load him up, and drop him off at the hospital. Simple as that. Little did I know I was in for a spiritual battle.

We got out of the truck and made our way to the caller. He was awake and breathing normally. His skin color was normal. He seemed alert, yet weak.

"What's going on today?" I asked.

He shrugged his shoulders and gradually turned his back toward me.

"Sir, do you want to tell me what's wrong today?"

He shrugged his shoulders again, gave me a disgusted look, and turned his back once more.

He was specifically avoiding me.

When one of my attendants attempted to questioned him, he responded without hesitation. The attendant proceeded to ask all the needed questions for assessment and received all the necessary answers.

I watched closely to see if the man would make eye contact with me. He never did. This was now obvious to everyone.

"I don't feel well. I want to go to get checked out at the hospital," he insisted, speaking directly to my attendant.

We elected to transport him. As we loaded him on the stretcher and into the ambulance, I got an idea. "When he's in the truck and seat-belted to the stretcher, I'll get down, look at him face to face, and find out what's really going on. He'll have to face me then," I reasoned.

That's exactly what I did. Once the patient was in the truck and securely seat-belted, I bent down, looked him square in the eye, and asked, "Why don't you tell me why you're not feeling well? It seems as if you don't want to talk to me."

He momentarily glared into my eyes. His blurry eyes reflected hate and bitterness. Sadistically he said, "Christians will burn in hell!"

He momentarily glared into my eyes. His blurry eyes reflected hate and bitterness. Sadistically he said, "Christians will burn in hell!"

I was stunned. I stumbled backward from my position at his side to the bench seat of the rescue truck. Totally awestruck by this man's statement, my emotions soared as an eerie silence gripped the truck.

First came fear. "This guy doesn't know me as a Christian. I haven't quoted scripture or made any reference to Christianity whatsoever in the short time I have been with him. And yet, he's attacking me as a Christian. What is this! Is there a power in his spiritual world that is battling the Lord of my spiritual world? And is this obvious power of darkness transferring its attack to the physical world and to the very speech of this man?"

I had no answer. All I knew was that I was in a state of shock.

Then, my emotions changed from fear to anger. "Who does this guy think he is, telling me 'Christians are going to burn in hell'? I'm going to get in his face, tell him he's a demon straight from hell, and get ready for a knock-down, drag-out, spiritual-turned-physical dogfight!"

Better judgment took over. I valued my job and wanted to keep it, and I didn't want to explain fresh injuries to the emergency room doctor for a "sick person" call.

"Lord, I've been insulted and attacked by Satan through this man! What should I say? What should I do? I want to say something, but what? And when?" I prayed.

My mind was preoccupied with what happened and what my strategic response should be, as I babbled words over the radio to the emergency room.

My partner, also notably stunned, measured vital signs and conversed minimally with the man. I maintained a position in the jumpseat behind him, keeping well out of sight.

My mind rambled on. "We'll be at the emergency room in less than a minute. I want to address this man before we exit the truck. I better think of something fast."

That minute seemed like seconds. We rolled onto the emergency room pad. The back doors opened. We prepared to unload the patient. I still didn't know what to say.

I prayed again as I helped to lower him out of the truck. "Lord, be with me."

Once again I bent down and looked him straight in the face and said, "Listen, man! Hell is a place where demons and people of Satan, not Christians, will burn forever and ever. You remember that, buddy!"

I expected the worse. I expected yelling, screaming, and bitter retorts. And I was ready to spiritually battle him over any response he might have. But he turned his head and looked away, saying nothing.

Relief encompassed my being. I felt assured that the Lord gave me that simple reply, especially since those words came only at the time I bent down and spoke.

I guess this vagrant needed a little clarification of hell's inhabitants — or at least the evil ruler in this man's dark spiritual world did. And he got it!

We received another call. I left the emergency room and the bitter man. To this day I am unaware of the man's outcome. But I will always remember the evil glare in his eyes as he shocked me with his demonic statement.

There must have been a pretty heated battle between our spiritual rulers on that day, when Ephesians 6:12 took on a very real meaning for this Christian paramedic.

A LIGHTER MOMENT

"There is an appointed time for everything . . ."

Mistaken Identity

Robbie is my identical twin brother. We are so alike that few people can tell us apart. One Sunday afternoon as Robbie transported the kids home on the church bus, one of the kids became suddenly ill, nearly passing out. One look at the pale, lethargic child prompted Robbie to stop at the nearby fire station to have the kid checked out by the paramedic on duty.

Unbeknown to Robbie, the nearest fire station was only a basic response station with emergency medical technicians. Robbie pulled into the station driveway. He honked the horn. One of the firefighter/EMT's came out.

"What's the problem?" he asked.

"One of my kids is sick," Robbie said. "He nearly passed out a little while ago."

Robbie and a couple more firefighter/EMT's walked to the back of the bus. The child was now resting and talking, but still looking pale and weak.

"What do you suppose is wrong with him? Could it be his heart or something?" Robbie asked.

The firefighters, obviously questioning Tommy Neiman's sanity, decided to confront Robbie before going any further. "Man, you're the paramedic. You're supposed to know what's wrong with him, so why are you asking us?

Are you messing with our minds?"

Robbie broke out laughing. "I'm Tommy's twin brother."

The kid laughed and immediately began to feel better. The guys just walked away, shaking their heads as Robbie drove off.

I met up with the firefighters several days later. They suggested I let Robbie work a shift for me.

I don't think so!

". . . A time to laugh."

ECCLESIASTES 3A: 1 AND 4B

CHAPTER 11

A Little "Brush" With Fire

"Therefore, take up the full armor of God, so that you will be able to resist in the evil day, and having done everything, to stand firm. Stand firm therefore, **having gird your loins with the truth,** *and* **having put on the breastplate of rightousness,** *and having* **shod your feet with the preparation of the gospel of peace;** *in addition to all taking up the shield of faith with which you were able to extinguish all the flaming arrows of the evil one. And take* **the helmet of salvation,** *and the sword of the spirit, which is the word of God."*

EPHESIANS 6:13-18

The south Florida coast has an abundance of cities complete with concrete, asphalt, and buildings coupled with beaches and boardwalks; yet there are also hundreds of square miles of inland residential wooded areas. These areas are of particular concern during the brush fire season — a season that traditionally begins in the early spring months when drier and cooler weather is combined with strong winds. These conditions frequently lead to woods and brush fires that are fast spreading, unpredictable, and treacherous.

As the only paramedic at the station, my responsibilities lay primarily with making medical calls and riding the rescue truck.

During one particularly dry brush fire season, the lieutenant altered my assignment. "It's you and me on Truck 5 today," he informed me.

Truck 5 was a brush truck at our station that was in a hot zone for woods fires. He felt this would give me an opportunity to renew my skills and get additional brush fire experience. I willingly complied.

After going over all the morning assignments he looked at me and said, "Go ahead and check out the truck. Make sure we have plenty of drinking water in the cooler."

"OK!" I replied as I started toward the truck room. Pushing the truck room door open, I thought, "All right! Maybe we'll get some action." I had no way of knowing that I was in for some truly major action that day.

I started my routine check of the brush truck. I checked the oil, radiator fluid, lights, siren, primer oil, and water level in the 500-gallon water tank. I pulled the truck outside and put the water pump in gear. I made sure it had good pump pressure by spraying a little water. And, could I help it if I pointed the hose in a direction where the mist hit the rescue truck guys?

"Sorry about that!" I teasingly said. "I don't get to squirt water too often, ya know, so I just had to take advantage of the opportunity."

As I finished checking out the truck, I was aware of a steady breeze in the dry morning air. I looked up. Not a cloud in the sky. The conditions were prime for brush fires. "Just maybe?" I thought.

The morning hours dragged on. The rescue guys went out on a couple of minor calls. I started to get a little bored as we began our routine station duties for that particular day — kitchen day. Cleaning out the fridge, washing the stove, scrubbing out the sink . . ." Man, I wished I'd stayed on rescue," I thought.

My thoughts were interrupted when central dispatch toned-out a nearby station for a reported grass fire near the interstate.

I threw my cleaning rag in the sink and ran outside to see if there was any smoke in the direction of the call. No smoke was visible, but the winds were beginning to pick up. Often a good breeze will cause the smoke to lie down, making it tough to see from any measurable distance.

I was anxious to know if there was ground smoke. "I know!" I said to no one in particular. " I'll climb up the radio tower in back of the station and see if I can see anything from up there." The other guys shook their heads at my starvation for action.

I scaled up about twenty feet of tower. I looked in the reported direction of the fire. Sure enough, there was smoke and a significant amount at that. I hurried down and ran inside. "I can see pretty good smoke lying low in that area, guys," I said excitedly.

My lieutenant shook his head rather negatively and said, "Well, I was hoping we would have a quiet morning."

"Not me," I thought to myself. "I'm ready to go!"

We waited for the dispatched brush truck to arrive on scene and give us a size up. But before that truck got to the fire, the tones once gain blared from central dispatch. A second grass fire was reported a mile to the north along that same interstate. Another brush truck was dispatched.

"What is going on?" we all wondered.

What we didn't know was that a man, traveling the interstate, was throwing out lit flares and intentionally starting woods fires! And he was successful not only in our county but in several other counties along the interstate as well.

When the first brush truck arrived at the initial fire, they radioed us. "We have about a half acre of fairly heavy brush involved in fire. I think we can handle this one."

I ran outside again to see if I could see any smoke from ground level. This time I could. "Probably both fires together in the same general direction are pushing up enough smoke," I thought. But in reality, both these fires were gaining in intensity. The winds were picking up, too.

I went back inside the station. The lieutenant on the second brush fire called in. "We have a similar size fire as the first. But a residence several lots downwind of this fire is in danger. Send another brush truck."

That meant us. Sure enough, as he finished his report, our station tones sounded. We were dispatched to assist the second brush truck. I ran out of the station like a kid out of school. I hurriedly bunkered out and jumped into the passenger side of Truck 5. My lieutenant, a twenty-year-plus veteran, grabbed his gear and strolled over to the truck. He threw his gear between us and hopped into the driver's seat. "You ready?" he said calmly.

"Yep, let's go." I tried to imitate his calmness as my adrenaline began to flow.

We radioed "going en route" and took off. Smoke was now very visible in the five miles of distance that separated us from the second reported fire. The siren button was on my side of the cab and I gave it all it was worth. We had one of those sirens that winds up to a high-screaming, almost deafening pitch, and believe me, I was keeping it in that zone.

"Are you having fun with that?" the lieutenant asked. "There's not a whole lot of traffic out here, ya know."

"Sorry about that! But I'm not having fun, lieutenant, I'm just having a blast!" I replied with a chuckle.

He smiled and shook his head.

Our eyes reverted to the smoke ahead of us. "It's really starting to put up some smoke," the lieutenant said. "Listen, Tommy, when we get in the area we're probably going to be directed by the battalion chief to stand by at the downwind residence. When we get there, just pull a line and stretch it between the house and the woods. If the woods are close to the house or they're really dense, we'll get another truck to stand by with us, okay?"

"Got it." I said confidently.

Just then we heard a radio transmission from one of the

trucks on scene. "Central, we're gonna need more help down here. We're getting a lot of spotovers and the winds are picking up!"

Hot airborne embers, carried by the increasing winds, were igniting additional fires where ever they landed. The situation was worsening. Almost simultaneously the first brush truck radioed a similar message, adding that their fire had jumped over a road and was starting on another area of vacant wooded lots.

This area was gettin' it! All of a sudden I felt a little more serious and a little less confident. "Lord, be with us this day," I quietly prayed in my heart. And in His awesome wonder, He certainly was.

We were less than halfway to the scene. The smoke show was now double in size and twice as dark. The lieutenant was really pushing it to get there. I continued to work the "get out of the way" button. We were now en route with a host of other brush trucks and pumpers. Our helicopter was dispatched to call strategy from above. But, even with all this equipment, by day's end some homes would be lost and others damaged.

When we arrived in the general area, smoke was everywhere. The strong winds continually shifted. I scanned over the area on the way to the scene. We continued to size up the area on arrival. Despite the smoky conditions, I noted we were in an area of mostly undeveloped residential blocks still in their natural wooded state, except for several homes scattered throughout the area. Many of these homes were on streets that hadn't been marked yet. We had our work cut out for us. We called into command. "Brush 5 to command, we're on scene in the area. Where do you want us?"

"Go ahead and position yourself at that exposure home just to the south of us," said command with notable urgency. "And get over there quick; the fire is pushing hard that way."

Within seconds we were positioned in front of the home. I grabbed the hose reel jumpline and ran it out along the side of the house. Smoke was already blowing through the woods and starting to fill the area where I positioned myself. Fortunately the woods bordering the residence were thin with no big trees growing up and over the dwelling. Nonetheless, there was enough fuel load for the fire to progress right up to, and ignite, this newly built wood frame house. Within seconds of our arrival, a bright orange head of fire became visible through the wooded brush. The brush truck engine revved up. My lieutenant charged my line. I bled the air out and waited for him to get over to me. A meager twenty-five feet or less lay between the side of the house and the woods.

Doubt coupled with apprehension overcame me. Could we handle this? Would we have enough water? I said a short prayer as I began to fight the fire.

My lieutenant crouched down beside me and said, "Let's get water on this head as soon as we can reach it, okay?"

"Okay," I replied. Within seconds we were shooting water through the woods into a thirty-to-forty foot head of fire that was beginning to bear down our way. I could feel white steamy soot blowing back on my helmet and face shield.

"Stay on it, Tommy!" the lieutenant yelled through the roar of the fire. "You're getting it!"

After three or four solid minutes of fight, only fragments of this head reached the property line. This house would make it. Smoke stains and a little peeled paint were nothing compared to what could have happened.

However, the day's challenges were only beginning. The wind shifts sent fire heads in numerous directions. Spot fires occurred everywhere! Dispatch continually gave out new locations as 911 calls kept pouring in on newly endangered structures. The number and intensity of the fires, the heavy smoke, and the lack of street signs made the situation seem futile.

We did get substantial help from the helicopter pilot who at times simply guided us, turn by turn, to the most threatened houses. Almost every piece of fire apparatus in our battalion was committed to this battle. After our initial save of that first exposure home, several pumpers arrived. They took over the responsibility of guarding dwellings from fast-moving heads. Our job was to try to knock down the spotovers that occurred when existing fires met a break, usually at a road. Our goal was to keep the next block of woods from being consumed. As we reached a block of woods, we wondered, "Is there a home in this area that could be at risk?"

We had no way of knowing where, or how many, homes were nestled in those wooded areas. The other brush trucks, located between us and that first reported brush fire, were trying to figure the same thing.

My responsibility was to ride on the back of our brush truck with the nozzle, then locate and hit the spotovers. Other brush firefighters were similarly engaged. Our feelings fluctuated from discouragement and frustration to the excitement of meeting a challenge. Many times after locating a spotover, we would hurry to it only to see it escalate into a large, unmanageable head. The heavy fuel load and wicked wind shifts made it impossible for us to approach the fire. We would then speed around to the back only to find the fire had jumped another road and was starting on the next block. We just couldn't get these fires under control. Fortunately, law enforcement evacuated most of the area and no one was hurt, but there were inevitable damages and losses.

I started to feel downhearted and beaten. "We can't stop it," I thought as we drove another two blocks ahead of the fire we were currently working.

We rolled to a stop in the middle of the block. My lieutenant jumped out. "Tommy, let's try it again, it should be here in a few minutes or so."

I noticed a little subsiding of the wind. My spirits lifted and with renewed confidence and a hint of cockiness I responded, "Lieutenant, this road is where the fire stops."

"Oh, really," he sarcastically replied.

"At least I hope so," I said under my breath.

I took my position on the back of the truck. We began traveling up and down the boundary road, waiting and looking for flying embers from the approaching fire. Within moments we saw some kindling about twenty yards away. We pulled up alongside it and my lieutenant put the pump in gear. "Hit it!" he yelled.

Ten seconds later that potential head was out. Over the next several minutes, we took care of three other little spotovers in similar fashion. "Maybe we can stop it at this road."

A large body of fire was fast approaching. I knew the result would be several spotovers at one time — spotovers that would be deeper into the woods on the opposite side of the road. Still, I felt confident we could knock them down and stop this part of the fire from claiming one more block.

I shouldn't have been so confident! Not only would this fire claim another block, it almost claimed me as well. You see, the spotovers did come and just as we thought, there were several of them that simultaneously ignited an area of tall grass well into the new block. Riding in the back with nozzle in hand, I banged on the back window and pointed toward the fresh fire. "I can handle it, Lieutenant! Let's try it."

"Are you sure, Tommy? You've got some heavy fuel close by!"

"Ya, I know, but the wind is moving it away from the brush so let's give it a shot."

"Okay, hang on!" he said.

We drove through a fifty-foot strip of high brush to get in a position to hit the burning grass. As we got into the midst of that high, volatile brush, a sudden strong wind shift occurred that turned the spotover area into a fierce fire head that literally engulfed the heavy brush all around us. I just knew I was gone! We were going to roast — truck and all! With flaming orange all around me, I slammed myself against the back windshield in a fetal position. "Oooooh," I yelled as I heard the truck rev hard and make full power.

My lieutenant made a very wise and fast decision. Instead of a right or left turn, which could have left us moving with and staying in that head of fire, he gunned us straight through to the previously burned spotover area.

I opened my eyes. "Praise God! I'm alive!" Steam was actually coming off me everywhere. "We could be dead," I reasoned to myself as we moved quickly away. And we certainly could have been. The deathly possibilities soared through my mind. The truck could have gotten stuck. It could have vapor-locked and stalled. I could have lost my position and balance and fallen into the flames. Any number of things could have happened. But, thank the Lord, He pulled us through.

We gave the block to the fire and retreated to the road. We stopped and my lieutenant jumped out. "Are you okay?"

"Uh, huh, I think so," I said, shaking. I did feel a stinging sensation around the top of my left ear and I could smell the odor

An allusive and wicked Florida brush fire:
Photo courtesy of the Fort Pierce Tribune, Florida.

of burned hair. Initially every part of me had been completely covered with turn-out gear, but when I balled-up against that back window, the collar of my coat and the underhood of my helmet separated just enough to catch a fiery dart. I never said a word, though. The top of my ear felt numb and the little strip of singed hair didn't hurt, but I was thankful to be alive and well.

The rest of the day was less eventful. We gained control of all the fires around nightfall and headed back to the station.

Tired and worn out, I lay my head on my bunk pillow that night and recalled the bright orange head of fire that I could see — even through tightly closed eyes — as we fled that terrifying and dangerous block. My prayers began that night with thanksgiving.

I thanked, and continue to thank, God for His blessed hand of protection. The thought of those threatening flames still scare me. I know that if it weren't for the Lord's presence, my life on earth would have been drastically changed or even ended. I also learned a valuable lesson from the Lord — a lesson about being properly geared out. Ephesians 6:11 says, "Put on the full armor of God, so that you may be able to stand firm against the schemes of the devil." In much the same way those flames hounded me, the flames of this world are hounding us as Christians. The only place where a dart of fire got in was an area that was left exposed. God used my protective fire gear to shield me against the torching flames. But a piece of that fire still found the little exposed area. Likewise, without God's full spiritual armor completely shielding us, we too are subject to Satan's fiery darts finding an exposed area.

Do you have all of God's protective gear — the belt of truth and the breastplate of righteousness? Are your feet shod with the Gospel? Have you taken the shield of faith, the helmet of salvation, and the sword of the spirit? God wants us to be fully geared out because He certainly knows we're always subject to having a " brush" with fire.

A LIGHTER MOMENT

"There is an appointed time for everything . . ."

A Bump And A Baby

A woman in labor came the call over dispatch. We routinely receive these calls, and with the relative proximity of hospitals in our district, there are few births in the field. We normally perform a quick check and give a nice ride to the OB unit while the expectant mom experiences occasional contraction pangs. This call was seemingly no different. The water had broken, but contractions were at least four to five minutes apart, and they lasted only a few seconds. This was going to be the lady's fifth child and her calm and relaxed manner indicated she was a pro.

"Think you can make it to the hospital?" I asked.

"If this baby doesn't come," she jokingly replied.

I assessed her status and then made a statement I'd have to eat later. "You have plenty of time."

We loaded her into the truck. I threw an IV in — per OB protocol — and witnessed another brief contraction, the first since our arrival at her home.

"We're ready," I yelled to my driver.

We took off for what I thought would be an early morning, uneventful ride to the hospital.

Not!!

About a minute into transport, she had another

brief contraction. "No big deal," I reasoned. All this movement probably triggered it and besides, it wasn't much of a contraction.

"You all right?" I asked.

"Yep," she replied.

We traveled at a decent speed down a main city street, only two major intersections from the area of the hospital. "The next two intersections are raised and we are in a weight-sensitive rescue truck," I casually explained, "so you'll experience two little bumps before we get to the hospital."

"No problem," she replied.

About fifteen seconds later when we approached that first bump, her casual demeanor suddenly changed. She let out a contraction groan just before we crossed the intersection that culminated in a yell upon exiting the intersection. A wide-eyed puzzled look flashed immediately on her face. Without hesitation, I pulled the sheet off of her.

"Wow!" I exclaimed. "We have a head."

With the OB kit on the bench next to me, I excitedly ripped it open and grabbed the suction bulb. I rushed the bulb to the protruding infant's head, suctioned out the nose and mouth, and witnessed the first breath of life. Aware of the urgency, my driver stepped up the pace. I clutched the baby's neck in my hand and said to the mommy, "All right. When you get the urge, push the rest of this…,"

Before I could finish, we hit the second intersection bump and this baby was practically shot-putted into my hands.

"Never mind. Mission completed. We have a little girl," I yelled out loud enough for all to hear. I wrapped our gift from God in a towel and handed her over to her mommy.

"Here is your wonderful gift from God, maam."

I grabbed the emergency room phone and told them we were only a few seconds away with an uncomplicated birth. We pulled into the hospital just as I was cutting the cord.

"I don't know why we're here, you're ready to go home now," I jokingly said.

With sweat beads still running down her face, she laid her head back and laughed, "You're right! Take me home!"

I opened the back doors and took hold of this new little arrival. Smiling at the woman, I said, "You bumped this one right into the world, didn't ya?"

". . . A time to laugh."

ECCLESIASTES 3A: 1 AND 4B

CHAPTER 12

A Missed Opportunity

". . . that most brethren, trusting the Lord because of my imprisonment, have far more courage to speak the word of God without fear."

PHILIPPIANS 1:14

The Apostle Paul is renowned for using all circumstances for the glory of God, including his imprisonment. While in prison, he encouraged all to be bold and share the truth in all situations and to have "more courage to speak the word of God without fear. "

The following rescue call is difficult for me to share. In so doing I am forced to reflect on a call that brings me both sadness and regret. But I feel I must share it. First, as a reminder for myself to never again let a critical opportunity slip eternally away. Second, in hopes it will encourage you to make the most of every opportunity God gives you to share His Son Jesus Christ.

The call came in, "a person experiencing back pains."

Sounded simple enough, maybe even a little boring. "A 911 call for back pain," I said to myself as I checked the map on the radio room wall. "Can't they get any more interesting than this?"

We jumped into the truck, hit the lights, and rolled toward the call location. Within four minutes we were on scene in front of an average house in a middle class neighborhood.

Not expecting anything too critical by the nature of the call, I grabbed our basic jumpbag and headed in. A middle-aged lady met us at the door.

"Sorry to bother you guys," she said apologetically. "But my husband's back is really hurting him and I thought it would be a good idea if you looked at him."

"What's your husband's name?" I asked as she guided us through the house.

"Richard," she said, "but he likes to go by Rick."

Rick was in the couple's bedroom lying flat across the bed. "Hi, guys, sorry about all the fuss," he said.

"No problem, sir," I replied. "What's going on with your back?"

"Well," he said with a strain in his voice, "I don't really know. I was fine when I woke up this morning. But all day at work I noticed an increasingly heavy pain in the middle of my back. I came home about an hour ago. I've been resting but it seems to be getting worse."

We sat him up.

"Have you had any prior back problems or recent injury?"

"Nothing," he responded. "Maybe it's just old age," he half-jokingly said.

His wife, who had left the room, came back in and mentioned they had been getting ready to go out to eat and do a little shopping.

Two teenage children were home and preparing for the family's outing. They came to the doorway. Rick looked at his wife and kids. "Go on ahead without me. I'm going to just take it easy." He looked back at us. "Just a little back strain, right?"

"I'm not really sure," I responded. "Let's get a set of vitals on you."

I motioned to one of my partners who proceeded to take his blood pressure while I palpated his back for any muscle stiffness or tenderness. "Let me know if I touch anything that hurts, okay?"

I didn't note any stiffness or any particular area of hurt.

"It feels like it's on the inside of my back," he said. "It's like a pressure pushing from the inside out."

I noticed his skin was somewhat sweaty and pale. I started to get a little nervous inside. "This guy actually looks shocky," I thought to myself.

I turned to my partner with an even keener interest in the patient's blood pressure. I saw my partner pump up the cuff again and could tell he was having a rough time getting a pressure. "I can't seem to hear anything," my partner stated.

"Let me try." I took the stethoscope and placed it to my ears. Before inflating the cuff, I felt Rick's wrist for a radial pulse. I could barely feel his faint, thready pulse. I knew now why the pressure was so difficult to obtain. It had to be low — very low. I demanded silence and stillness while I quickly inflated the cuff and listened intently. "Fifty-six over thirty-eight — normal is one-twenty over eighty." His blood pressure was low, deathly low. But why?

My adrenaline kicked into gear. I knew something was drastically wrong. Then it hit me what this could be. As calmly as possible, I told Rick his blood pressure was seriously low. I laid him back down.

"Rick, I need to unbutton your shirt and look at your stomach."

My suspicions were confirmed. He had a hardened area in his upper abdomen that was gently, but discernibly, pulsating.

"This guy has an abdominal aortic aneurysm that is dissecting," I thought to myself assuredly. An abdominal aortic aneurysm is a condition in which a weak part in the wall of the aorta, the largest artery in the body, balloons out under pressure until it ruptures. The pulsation in his stomach was actually his aorta which had ballooned out from his spine all the way to where it could be felt as a pulse in his upper abdomen. He was literally bleeding to

No one cared about shopping. Even the back pain was out of the picture. A value for continued life was all that now mattered.

death on the inside.

We needed to shift to into high gear, but I didn't want to terrify Rick and his family. Still, they needed to know how serious things were.

I hastily, and more aggressively, asked Rick if he had any known medical problems.

His wife, noting seriousness in my sudden change of demeanor, said, "He's always been healthy. Why are you asking this? What's going on?"

I looked at Rick. Addressing both of them I said, "I think you're having some major bleeding inside from a large, possibly ruptured, vessel. We need to go to the hospital — immediately!"

The kids, still lingering in the doorway, heard my diagnosis. The whole atmosphere and plans in this household changed. No one was thinking about eating. No one cared about shopping. Even the back pain was out of the picture. A value for continued life was all that now mattered.

My two partners, aware of the assessment, were two steps ahead of me. One of them went for the stretcher while the other began assembling and readying a large IV. I instructed him to make that two IV setups.

Rick seemed quiet — as if in denial. Then he looked up and said, "I haven't needed to see a doctor for anything in years. I've been good health-wise. I just can't understand this."

"Sometimes there is not a whole lot of warning with these things," I replied compassionately while lifting him onto the stretcher. "They just happen."

Rick's wife quickly came to his side, with tears forming. She told him she loved him and that she and the kids would meet him at the hospital.

As we rolled the stretcher outside, the kids hugged him, saying, "I love you, Daddy."

My spirit was touched as I, for that brief moment, let a wave of their love for him brush up against me.

But aggressive patient treatment and stabilization were needed. I was determined to get this guy's blood pressure up and stabilize him so he would have a shot at making it to the operating room. Even before the stretcher was in the truck, I had his feet propped up in a shock-preventing position. Within ninety seconds of being in the rescue truck he was on high flow oxygen, had a quick-look EKG, and a large bore needle IV established and running wide open.

"Go!" I yelled to my driver who was waiting for the word.

Rick was pale and sweating profusely. A quick blood-pressure check by way of palpation showed a shaved reading of 50/p. It was too low for a lower reading. "I've got to get this pressure up," I thought.

Even with only four minutes of transport time, another wide-open IV was imperative, but the hospital needed to be informed of this priority one patient. An EMT partner was riding in the back with me. I directed him to radio the emergency room while I took on the always difficult effort of getting an IV established in a rough-riding truck.

Praise the Lord, the attempt was successful and more fluid could be pushed. I heard the EMT's transmission and felt the accuracy of his patient assessment description would prompt the readiness for our arrival. We were now a minute out. Time to see if the 700 cc's of saline fluid had done anything to raise his blood pressure. Pulling into the ER apron, his pressure was 80/40.

"Better," I stated aloud in Rick's direction. "Rick, we're at the hospital. They're probably going to take some quick X-rays and give you some blood so they can get you ready for surgery on that ruptured vessel, okay?"

Rick nodded weakly as we rushed him though the emergency room doors.

A full complement of ER nurses, a portable X-ray crew, and two physicians were standing by in expectation of our arrival. We transferred Rick from the ambulance stretcher to the hospital gurney. I stepped back and gave the primary ER doctor a brief summary on our patient's current condition.

He responded with a quick "okay" and disappeared into the crowd of attendants at Rick's bedside.

I took a couple of deep breaths and headed over to the report table. I sat down, thinking that the last ten minutes felt more like ten seconds. Rick's chances weren't good. I couldn't help but wonder, "Where does this guy stand with the Lord?" I looked again at his treatment area some twenty-five feet away and noted the continued chaos. All too methodically, I pulled out my run report and began to write, distracted from the crucial spiritual question I had just asked myself. All too suddenly, my focus was on producing an impressive narrative for my run report rather than dwelling on a potential spiritual need that was by far a million times more important.

One of the doctors came over and asked me if the family was on their way. This was a fortunate, or more accurately a God-sent interruption, that stopped my writing. After answering his question, I asked for his opinion about Rick's condition. "What do you think, Doc?" I somewhat optimistically asked.

He looked at me, took a breath, and stated, "He's got less than a five percent chance even if he makes it to surgery — realistically about two percent"

I let my chin sink down onto my hand as he walked back to the treatment area. "I really need to share with this guy," I told myself as I looked over at the treatment stall that was loaded with people. I knew that I could go right to his side and talk to him if I really wanted to. But, cowardly, I backed out and resigned myself to the wimpy thought of, "Oh, there's too many people, maybe I'll just wait a bit."

I started writing again.

Within a couple of minutes some commotion got my attention. Down the hallway, toward their loved one's treatment area, came the family accompanied by several others. Grave concern covered their faces. I watched them intermingle with the health care people and close in on Rick. Tears filled his wife's eyes as she talked to one of the doctors. Her love for Rick was apparently deep and sincere. Yet I saw no prayer, no one carrying a Bible, no family member seeking a nurse to call a pastor or even the hospital chaplain. I recalled their home that bore no evidence that Jesus Christ was Lord of anyone's heart there.

"I just have to talk to this man," I reaffirmed to myself. I planted my feet under the chair and stood up. I looked at Rick being hugged by his daughter and hesitated. Again my weak, earthly mind overruled my spiritually discerning heart.

"Maybe I shouldn't interrupt their family time," was the cop-out excuse that set me back down in my chair. "I'll just give them a few minutes and then I'll go over there regardless."

I looked down at a particular part of my report. "I'll just knock this section out real quick."

I started writing. My focus on Rick's spiritual need left for what I thought was only a split second. But in that supposed split second I lost my opportunity to share with a man facing eternity. When I looked up from that piece of paper, I saw Rick being rapidly wheeled away. My opportunity — make that opportunities — were over.

I stood. I looked wide-eyed at the nurse. "Now?" I exclaimed.

"They had to try now, while they had a shot," she said.

"I was the one that needed to try now, while I had a shot," I thought to myself. But my time had come and was now gone. My heart sank.

We finished our responsibilities and headed toward the truck. I looked one more time at Rick's treatment area stall which was now empty and quiet. "Lord, please bring him through," I prayed under my breath.

But Rick's time had come. Before we made it back to the station, Rick died in surgery. Simply stated, my intention had been just that, only an intention. The opportunity to share Christ died at that report table.

Lord may I never again have to recall such a crucial missed opportunity.

Writing about this call is painful. But it made me determined to never again let such a golden opportunity to share the Lord slip needlessly away.

How about you? As a child of God, have you been prompted by the Holy Spirit to share the love of our wonderful Savior and yet balked at the calling?

Satan diverts us with rationalizations. "Well, maybe next time," or "They probably won't believe, anyway." But the truth is, as I experienced with Rick, there might not be a next time.

In Rick's case I inwardly knew there wasn't going to be a next time. And yet I let excuses such as "There are too many people at Rick's bedside" and "I don't want to interrupt their family time" keep me from sharing Jesus, His peace, and the eternity He offers.

Absolutely nothing should have kept me from going directly to Rick — even in the midst of his family — and finding out where he stood with the Lord. And yet something did — my apprehension, my fears, my anxieties. All were weak devil-ridden excuses that I let grieve and hinder the spiritual work that God was wanting to do through me.

I hope you won't let Satan keep you quiet when prodded by the Holy Spirit to share your testimony with someone. May you and I always be true and obedient to the spirit's calling, and "have far more courage to speak the word of God without fear," for it may be the only opportunity we have to share Christ before a person goes unexpectedly to eternity.

A LIGHTER MOMENT

"There is an appointed time for everything . . ."

The Station 2 Squirrel

Animals are notorious for finding homes at fire stations. They seem to create a keen yet temporary interest, as well as a sense of motherly concern, on the part of the firefighters. Over the years I've seen an array of animals seek temporary shelter in a fire station. Dogs and cats make up the majority of these vacationers. But we've also had birds, raccoons, armadillos, and the like. We even had a large python hanging out our front door one night after we returned from a fire alarm. Naturally we took it in, until a gentleman came and claimed it. But of all the animals that have performed unknowing fire department duty, the most memorable one is the Station 2 Squirrel. This little guy earned high honors among fireman. His picture was, and I believe still is, on the Station 2 wall.

My encounter with the Station 2 Squirrel occurred unexpectedly in my first year on the fire department. I had been moved out to Station 2, and after cleaning the bathrooms — a rookie's primary station job — I walked into the kitchen. There in the middle of the dinner table was a squirrel. He was just sitting there eating a big walnut.

I stopped in my tracks and tried to get this picture into proper perspective. Three of our guys sat at the table buried in the newspaper or eating cereal. Everyone, including the squirrel, was silent, still, and respectfully doing their thing. I tried to be "business as usual" and mosey over and get a bowl of cereal. I casually said, "Who's the visitor?"

"Where?" one of the veterans responded with his head still buried in the sports page.

I began wondering if that last unoccupied bunk in the back was really mine or not. Finally the guys came back to life, the squirrel finished his walnut and bounced around a bit, and I heard all about this unique creature.

As my month's stay at Station 2 progressed, my affection grew in the warmth and delight of this little critter. We never really gave him a name but merely said the "kik, kik" sound to get his attention. Most mornings, the on-duty shift would open the screenless back kitchen window of the station. The barbecue grill was positioned right outside, so our fun-loving friend would jump on it, up to the windowsill, and take a studious look inside. Then, after feeling comfortable and probably weeding out the avid hunters of the department, he would jump down onto the kitchen counter and follow it around the corner, jumping over the sink and the stove burners in the process. Then he would jump to the floor, scamper to the dinner table, and using the nearest chair, vault himself up to the middle of the table where he would wait expectantly for breakfast. And he never left hungry. He seemed to trust everyone, at least those with blue uniform shirts on, and I had him walking on my arms and shoulders almost immediately.

Especially neat was the way the other squirrels responded to him and he to them. Our friend would always leave with a nut of some type for the road. Many of his cowardly squirrel buddies waited in the tree by the window, gazing in and anxiously awaiting their brave friend's return. When he arrived, they trounced all over him and chased him all around. Then, as if to throw mud in their faces, he would return to the windowsill and eat his "nut for the road" in full view of his jealous buddies.

The Station 2 Squirrel was undoubtedly quite the character. We enjoyed his antics shift after shift. Then one day, he didn't show up. There were squirrels in the back trees, but no special one jumped up to the windowsill. We continued to anticipate his arrival all morning and wondered what was hindering him. Then we got a call. We hurriedly exited the station and headed on our way, but not so quickly that we failed to notice two fluffy tails protruding from car-squished animals about 500 feet down the road.

"No," I thought. We passed by them, realizing these animals were both squirrels that had been killed. "That might have been our little buddy," I told my partner.

"Ya, I know," he replied dejectedly.

Upon returning, we told the guys about what we saw, hoping that neither of the squished squirrels was our morning companion. But as each day passed and no squirrel adorned our breakfast table, we concluded the Station 2 Squirrel hadn't learned to look both ways before crossing the street.

The Station 2 Squirrel was a neat little character. He left quite an impression on the guys and really helped lighten the atmosphere at this busy station. And, yes, I did have a bunk to sleep in.

". . . A time to laugh."

ECCLESIASTES 3A: 1 AND 4B

CHAPTER 13

An Ungrateful Choker

"Oh that men would praise the Lord for His goodness, and for His wonderful works to the children of men."

PSALM 107:8 KJV

During the past fourteen years of my career in fire and rescue, though I've never kept count, I would estimate I have responded to literally thousands of calls ranging from false alarms to life-sustaining emergency calls. On the latter, it is usually the combined teamwork of the rescue crew and the emergency room professionals that makes the difference in whether a patient survives or not. But included among those responses classified as definite emergencies are the rare calls where life and death are only split seconds apart — where only an immediate action performed on scene saves a life. I praise God for blessing me with the gratification and overwhelming joy of being on several of these calls. However, I am humbled by the realization that a physical life saved is only temporary. A far more important life saved is a spiritual life, and only Jesus can do that. No matter how gratifying it is to save a physical life, if a non-believing person is snatched from death only to live out the remainder of his or her life without accepting Christ, the life saved doesn't mean much. At least from an eternal perspective. How awesome it is, though, when a person narrowly misses physical death and as a result comes to a saving knowledge of Jesus Christ.

When God uses me to help save a physical life, I give Him praise. When He uses me to share His truth, and that sharing helps lead someone to a believing knowledge of Jesus Christ, I am overwhelmed with joy, praise, and the realization that all honor and glory goes to God.

But on these rarest of all the calls, like the one that follows, my heart cries out as King David's did in Psalm 107:8: "Oh that all men would praise the Lord for His goodness."

It had been a busy day. Since 7:30 a.m. one call after another had come in. Nothing major, but nonetheless legitimate calls. At 1:00 in the afternoon we still hadn't made it back to the station. I was hungry but realized we were in for one of those long, busy, and perhaps lunchless shifts. "If the radio would just be quiet long enough for us to get back, grab some grub, and sit down for fifteen minutes, I'll be ready for anything," I thought.

The radio didn't keep quiet and my lunch was postponed once again — all because someone else's lunch wasn't being eaten properly.

"Central to Rescue 2, please copy a call," the radio blared. "You have a choking victim at the Palm Avenue Mental Health Facility. Patient is unresponsive and not breathing."

"Copy Central," my driver replied. "En route from Highland and 39th." We hit the lights and siren.

"This is a real one," I thought as my heart raced with excitement. "This is what it's all about."

Divinely, this call came in with our truck only four short blocks from the mental health facility. We would be there in ninety seconds or less. I yelled to my EMT in the back jumpseat, "Donny, get the airway bag out and grab my laryngoscope and the McGill forceps." This would be my primary equipment if the call description was accurate. "Oh God, let me be able to do this," I inwardly prayed. I took a deep breath and could feel the Lord taking away the jitters rushing through my veins. His peace passes all understanding. Amen!

We came to a harsh stop at the breezeway of the facility. If the call was for a patient, it would mean entering through a minimum of two sets of security doors.

My partner, also aware of the security measures, blurted out, "They better have those doors open!" It's funny how we were thinking the same thought.

Fortunately, the doors were open. Fully loaded with med boxes and airway bags, we passed through both doors. The second door led into the cafeteria/social hall where, in the distance, twelve to fifteen people formed a crowded circle around a figure lying flat on the floor. The care worker, who let us in, hurried along with us. "One of the lady patients just started choking while eating her lunch," she said.

We approached.

The circle gave way, revealing another care worker straddling the downed lady and administering abdominal thrusts in relentless desperation.

"Anything come up?" I anxiously asked.

"No," she cried.

The patient looked to be about forty. Her face was an eerie ashen blue. Her body was pale and lifeless.

"How long has she been down?" I asked.

"I don't know, probably close to five minutes. I can't get any air down her," she responded.

"Donny, give me the laryngoscope and forceps," I said. A laryngoscope is a piece of medical equipment that has a handle and adjustable tongue depressor-like blade that houses a small, bright light. It is used primarily for placing breathing tubes directly into the lower airway for direct access to the lungs. Hence, it is also great for removing foreign objects. I grabbed the laryngoscope and McGill forceps, an eight-inch tweezers-like instrument. I instructed the care worker to stop. I needed the patient to be still so I could try to get a good visual. I inserted the laryngoscope blade and exposed her trachea. Just beyond her vocal cords was an object that appeared to be a breaded mass. It was about the size of a large gumball and completely obstructed her passage. With the laryngoscope in place I inserted the forceps to almost their maximum reach. Praise God! I was able to take hold of the entire mass and remove it from her throat.

I heard a quiet, cautious, chorus of "All right's!" from the crowd. They seemed to realize, as did I, that it could be too late.

The patient made no attempt to breathe once the object — a hardened clump of peanut butter and bread — was out. I immediately grabbed the resuscitative bag and began ventilating her with 100% oxygen. A good chest rise ensured that an air exchange was at least taking place. But would it be too late?

"Check a pulse, Donny," I cried out.

"I think I got one, but it's real faint," he returned.

"Maybe," I thought and prayed.

However, there was still no effort on her part to breathe. I had my other assistant take over ventilating while I took a stethoscope and listened to her lungs. "Good air movement," I called out. "Let's get a quick look at her EKG rhythm and move out."

Her heart rate was fast as expected, but absent of lethal dysrythmias. Still, her pupils were only minimally responsive. "Brain dead," I thought. "She was just down too long without oxygen," I reasoned.

We placed her on the stretcher and wheeled her through the two sets of doors toward our waiting unit.

But wait a second, between two of my ventilations, I noticed a small chest rise. Remarkably, within a couple of seconds, there came another

> *But wait a second, between two of my ventilations, I noticed a small chest rise. Remarkably, within a couple of seconds, there came another small breathing attempt. "She's trying to breathe, guys."*

small breathing attempt. "She's trying to breathe, guys," I excitedly said.

I continued to assist with her still-inadequate attempts at ventilation. We placed her in the truck, started an IV, and quickly put her back on the cardiac monitor. Her heart rate was less rapid and her facial color was a 180-degree turn from five minutes prior. "Hallelujah, there's a chance," I thought.

By the time we were en route, she was showing good chest rise with increased respiration. A few moments later I noticed her eyes flickering.

"Ginny. Do you hear me? Ginny? . . .Ginny?"

She briefly opened her eyes each time I yelled her name. I quit ventilating through the airway bag and, since her breathing rate and depth were adequate, I put her on an oxygen mask. I couldn't believe what I was seeing! Within two minutes of the five-minute trip to the hospital, Ginny started spontaneously opening her eyes. She was also trying to mumble through the oxygen mask. By the time I encoded a brief report to the ER, this woman was grabbing at the IV.

I grabbed her hand. "Leave that in," I instructed gently.

She then went for the oxygen mask. Again I intervened. She resisted as she yanked on the mask. "Get this thing off me," she insisted.

"At least we know she's able to talk," I said discreetly to my EMT.

He just grinned — probably as startled as I was by her progress. I yielded to her wish since she obviously wasn't done talking.

"Why is my throat hurting?" she continued.

My partner informed her about what had happened as I smilingly looked on. I interjected, saying, "And thank God we were able to get it out."

I expected a total change in attitude. Was I surprised when instead of gratitude, the bullets really flew!

"Well, you should have done a better job," she responded as she maneuvered her mouth around. "I think you loosened one of my teeth!"

I couldn't believe her response. "Maybe she does have some brain damage," I humorously thought to myself. "Does this woman know the predicament she was in? Does she know how very close to death she was? "

I calmly reiterated what happened as I took her blood pressure. Her response was a very cold, "Thank you."

"No," I replied back. "You need to thank the Lord for allowing us to be so close to your facility. If we had gotten the call and responded from our station, you would be dead."

She remained indifferent as we arrived at the hospital. While we were unloading her, she glanced at the IV and said, "Well, if I'm OK, why is that thing in my arm?"

"Oh well," I sighed as we took her inside and transferred her to one of the treatment area gurneys.

"You got my encode, didn't you?" I said to the report nurse.

"Yes," she responded. "Sounds like a great job, Tommy. How is she doing?"

"Well, as you can see, her color is good, her vitals are stable, no EKG abnormalities, and her lungs are clear."

"Great!" the nurse exclaimed as I headed down the hall.

Turning, I looked back at the nurse and said, "She's just a little bit ungrateful, though."

The nurse didn't hear me, for Ginny captured her attention with complaints about her loose tooth and sore throat.

I never expected a response like Ginny's. Even though this woman was temporarily being treated for emotional problems, she seemed intelligent and bright. Couldn't she comprehend what happened? Couldn't she see God's mighty hand in the circumstances that surrounded this ordeal? There's no doubt in my mind that she was knowledgeable of the facts. They were clear in her mind but cold and darkened in her heart. How could anyone be like that when something so wonderful was done for them?

Then a thought crossed my mind. Isn't this how we as children of God sometimes respond to Him? John 3:16 tells us that God sent His only Son, Jesus Christ, to save our lives not only temporarily, but forever! And yet, like that ungrateful choker, groaning and whining about minor and temporary inconveniences of the flesh keeps us from focusing on Christ and experiencing His love and mercy through what HE did for us. A path of pure gold and eternal life awaits all who accept the saving blood of Christ.

"Oh," I thought as Psalm 107:8 crossed my mind. "If only people would praise God for His goodness. If only they would focus on Him and not allow the little inconveniences of life to distract them. Maybe then a call like this could have ended with the saving of both a physical and a spiritual life."

Have you ever been like the ungrateful choker? I know I have.

If so, we need to focus on Christ and "praise the Lord for His goodness and for His wonderful works," and fewer complaints will come to mind.

A LIGHTER MOMENT

"There is an appointed time for everything . . ."

Jokes 'R' Us

If a person wanted to write a manual on practical jokes, the average fire station should not be overlooked. Firefighters frequently have idle time on their hands, and what better way to spend this time than finding clever ways to get the best of a new comrade.

The primary target is the rookie, and a new guy's first day means nothing less than a barrage of practical jokes. My first shift was no different.

On that memorable first day, I found guys jumping out of the large trash dumpster when I was chosen to take the garbage out at 10:00 at night, and that was just the beginning. Clean-up duties completed, I jumped in the shower, and soaped up just as the tones went off. I wasn't about to miss a call on this, my first shift, so I jumped out, still half covered with soap, threw on my jumpsuit, ran to the pole and, because I was wet, didn't exactly slide down with a controlled grip. Instead I literally flew down the pole trying desperately, but awkwardly, to slow my descent. I hit the bottom padding on the truck room floor. Loud laughter accompanied my bump. "False alarm, Tommy."

I laughed and secretly hoped this was the end of the pranks.

Wrong!

We went back upstairs and things chilled out a bit.

Then, one of them told me about a dish that didn't get washed and would I kindly take care of it before going to bed. (Yes, rookies get dish duty, too.) They acted so serious and matter-of-fact that I really thought I had missed a dish. Besides, I reasoned that the jokes had now ended. Well, I went to the sink, hit the lever to turn the water on, and instinctively jumped back as I was hit with a hard stream of water from the side sprayer. They had rubber-banded it wide open. Another laugh on the new guy's initiation day.

Things finally settled down, and one by one the guys went back into the dorm to go to bed. Within a few minutes I was the only one left in the day room. Again, I gullibly reasoned that these guys had had their fun and now they were going to bed. Not wanting to be the oddball, I figured I'd do the same. I grabbed my boots, walked back, and gently opened the dorm room door. I stepped inside. The dorm was deathly quiet and pitch black. "Man, these guys don't fool around when it's sack time," I thought. I knew I dared not turn on any lights, so I waited for my eyes to adjust before moving. All I needed to do was stumble over someone's bed, land on him in it, and destroy the rest of my career!

After a few seconds I slowly crept toward the general direction of my bed. The room was big and it accommodated twelve bunks. The last thing I wanted to do was blindly tap the wrong one, which would be another career-ruining move! But I felt confident as I neared what I knew was my bed. I brushed my leg up against the foot end and could tell by the material I had made it. "Home free," I thought.

Still unable to see, I guided myself around the side of my bed and leaned over to quietly place my boots on the floor. But before I stood up, a scary animal roar rang out behind me as I was pushed onto my bunk. Not only was I startled to death, but I landed on a hard human-like figure buried underneath my cover, which scared me even more. I jumped off to the sounds of massive laughter in the room.

I hit the bed light and pulled off the covers to unveil the rescue mannequin. "Lord, let this be all," I prayed boldly out loud.

Finally, I fell asleep. The rest of the night was call free, and more importantly, practical joke free except, of course, for the gentle coating of flour under the covers that added one more round of laughter in the morning before shift change.

". . . A time to laugh."

ECCLESIASTES 3A: 1 AND 4B

CHAPTER 14

My Motorhome Is On Fire

"Let us hold fast the confession of our hope without wavering, for He who promised is faithful; and let us consider how to stimulate another to love and good deeds, not forsaking their own assembling together, but encouraging one another; and all the more as you see the day drawing near."

HEBREWS 10:23-25

I arrived for duty at 7:20 a.m. for the 7:30 shift change. However, when the "C" shift crew and I arrived, we were surprised to find the station empty. Both the engine and the rescue truck were gone. An odd feeling overcame me as I walked through the vacant truck room in uniform. We had a full shift of guys ready for duty, but no trucks to respond in.

The bay doors were open. Not a customary practice. Normally when leaving the station for a call, the crew secures the doors and station. They must have just departed — and hurriedly at that. I went inside the station and quickly called dispatch. "What did "B" shift have?" I inquired. "They departed three minutes ago," came the response, "for a serious wreck."

Dispatch filled me in on the details. The location was a desolate area near the county line. Florida Highway Patrol advised that a pickup truck with five people riding in the back cab lost control, flipped over several times, and ejected all five. Our trauma hawk and the neighboring Okeechobee County were responding.

"Man," I thought, "I was three minutes away from an exciting call." I would never wish misfortune on anyone, but when a need such as this arises, it is always disappointing to be left behind. With all the trucks gone, I knew I would remain idle for a good part of the morning.

But God had other plans for me. A battalion chief stopped by and we had, I later discovered, a divinely appointed conversation. I was in need of encouragement, and he was God's selected encourager. During this time of fellowship we talked about sharing and comforting our fellow brothers and sisters in Christ. The battalion chief shared how God specifically led him to help and encourage a new believer who now faced battles in his new walk. As our conversation level deepened I felt the chief's need to share, as well as his need be encouraged, too. When he left, I knew God had placed me exactly where he wanted me that morning. Consequently, my disappointment in not being on the earlier call slowly subsided.

The guys returned about 10:30 a.m. "You guys missed it!" I overheard one of them say.

"Oh well," I sighed, but again I reflected on the time of fellowship and encouragement of a brother in Christ and easily accepted their exciting details of the call.

The usual shift change procedures followed. We signed-off drug logs and restocked used supplies. About fifteen minutes later, the shift supervisor called. "Bring the spare rescue truck to the Central Fire Station. We are going to put a full inventory of equipment on it and return it to service at another station," he explained.

"Boring, boring, boring," I thought.

Another station was assigned to cover our response area while we would be at Central taking care of this three-hour detail.

We loaded up and headed to Central. "Now I'm sure there will be another exciting call just as soon as we get to Central," I sarcastically reasoned.

We arrived at Central and began the tedious task of transferring and logging a full inventory of everything right down to individual bandages.

This shift wasn't going anything like expected. "Why couldn't they have gotten this whim yesterday — or even tomorrow when we weren't on duty?" I half-seriously joked with the other guys — okay, maybe seventy-five percent seriously.

We joked back and forth, talked of personal and departmental matters, and began to uplift each other as we went about the necessary, yet menial, transfers and labeling of items.

"Only a couple more to go," I shared encouragingly when we reached the last few items to be swapped.

Just then the speakers at Central sounded and their station was dispatched to a fire just ten blocks away. A man had frantically called 911 exclaiming, "My motorhome is on fire and it's very close to my house."

I watched in envy as the Central guys bunkered out, loaded up, and headed to 904 Emily Ave. I shook my head and stepped back into the cab of the rescue truck, listening to the bellowing sirens fade in the distance. But even before the sounds of sirens were completely gone, the truck room intercom gave way to dispatch. "Rescue 11, can you do back-up rescue response on the call?"

"Yesss!" I yelled excitedly. I instructed Paul, my EMT, to just throw the remaining items anywhere and get in the truck. I grabbed the truck radio microphone and told dispatch we could respond and would be en route momentarily.

Ordinarily we would not have been dispatched, but Central's rescue truck was on another call and the next closest station's rescue truck was also tied up. It is standard operating procedure to dispatch a rescue truck with an engine response, so this gave us the unusual opportunity to respond despite being a long distance from Rescue 11's call zone. Wasting no time, we sounded our sirens and pulled out of Central. Immediately we saw a large column of black smoke in the distance.

"It looks like it could be going good!" I said emphatically.

I looked over at Paul. The boredom of the last three hours was replaced with anticipation, anxiety, and unanswered questions. Were there people caught in the flames? Was anyone in, or near, that motor home? What about the vehicle's fuel and propane tanks! Would we be able to contain the flames and save the house?

Within a minute we heard Engine 1 radio that they were on scene. They gave their assessment as a large motorhome fully involved in the front end. In addition, they stated a nearby exposure (the house) was starting to be involved as well. "We might have a house fire!" I thought.

Navigating the last three or four blocks was difficult. The heavy surge of traffic near the fire area slowed us down. A great many spectators, in car and on foot, also decided to respond. They were in a slow, deliberate mode as they neared the block of the fire, determined not to miss one moment of action. Many chose to ignore the tones of our loud siren.

Paul rolled his window down and yelled into the crowd, "MOVE! MOVE!"

But to no avail, the crowd was lost in its own spectator world.

Paul had one thing on his mind — as does any rookie firefighter — that almighty nozzle! Since we were responding in a rescue truck, I knew our first priority would be patient care. Then, if there were no injuries, we would have a chance at firefighting duties. I'm sure Paul was praying for no injuries.

We arrived at the corner of Emily Ave. To our delight, a police cruiser had blocked off the street from traffic. We slowed down enough to let the officer move aside. Once we got past him, the involved motorhome came into sight. It was just five houses

The meager remains of the pastor's motorhome.
Photo courtesy of the Fort Pierce Tribune, Florida

down, and it was cooking. Flames consumed and lit up the entire forward end. The smoke was heavy and black, making it impossible to tell if the house adjacent was on fire.

We rolled to a stop about 100 feet behind Engine 1. We gave a quick "on scene" to dispatch. Central's engine company strategically directed hose streams between the house and motorhome. As I jumped out of our truck, an officer with Engine 1 called out our assignment. Paul was to bunker out and join the firefighting effort, a command that was music to his ears. I was directed to examine the owner of the motorhome.

The owner, an older gentleman, was standing in the front yard, closely studying every detail of the effort to quench this fire and save his house. Evidently he had tried to do a little garden hose firefighting before Engine 1 arrived, and as a consequence suffered some minor burns. I walked past the action-packed driveway, through the front yard, and directly to my patient.

"You all right, sir?" I asked.

"Ya! I think so," he responded. "Just a couple of spots on my hand and arm where I felt a little heat," he continued. "I just can't believe this! We're supposed to be taking this thing on vacation tomorrow!"

There was redness on the top of the man's hand and in the biceps area of his arm. He was visibly shaken and mildly hyperventilating — and understandably so. I turned and joined him in his studious gaze at the fire suppression effort. The guys had now knocked most of the fire down and it was clear that the house was no longer in jeopardy.

"Sir, why don't you come over to the truck with me so I can check those red areas and get you out of this smoke and heat."

It was high noon. The temperature on this searing summer day was nearly 100 degrees with an accompanying high humidity. We walked back to Rescue 11. I sat him down on the bench seat and quickly grabbed a towel from the cabinet.

"I'm sorry about your motorhome," I said as I dabbed his sweaty forehead and face dry.

"Ya, I know, I just can't believe this," he stated. "I just started it up to check everything. Then, as I looked in through the engine housing, I noticed a little fire! I ran for the hose and it wouldn't quite reach. Can you believe that! Next thing you know, the whole engine's on fire! Then I ran in and called you guys." He rolled his eyes and sighed.

I took sterile water and began to cleanse the reddened areas on his arm and hand. Something about his composure and voice seemed familiar and I felt an immediate hint of commonality.

"I guess the Lord didn't want you to take this particular motorhome on that trip tomorrow," I said casually as I attended to his burns.

He gave me a unique, yet imploring look in response.

"Yes, I believe you're right," he said.

"What kind of work are you in?" I ventured to ask.

"I'm a pastor."

"Oh, man, that's great," I responded. "I'm a pastor of a new mission church that is meeting on Okeechobee Road," I added.

He told me the name of his church and as we spoke of mutual acquaintances, he began to calm down.

"Your vitals are stable and your burns are not in need of further medical attention," I stated positively. "I think you're going to make it."

He grinned a little and nodded, "Yep! I sure am. Wish I could say the same for the motorhome, though."

I gathered the needed patient information, all the time thinking about how God arranged for one pastor to hook up with another pastor in a time of need. Thoughts of my talk with the battalion chief also crossed my mind as this pastor and I conversed freely about Christ's love for us and how in difficult times such as this, He is always there. We spoke of church matters, of our common call to preach God's word, and our special, yet tough, desire to "fight fires" from the pulpit each Sunday morning. God gave me an opportunity to encourage this fellow brother in a time of need and in turn, his words were encouraging to me.

As I completed his treatment and the paperwork, his wife came to the back door of the truck. She climbed inside and sat down next to her husband. She wasn't injured but, like her husband, she was hot, upset, and in need of reassurance that things were under control. I placed a towel around her neck as she looked into her husband's eyes and said, "Are you all right?"

"Yes," he replied with conviction.

Her anxiety subsided.

They spoke awhile. Confident that his wife was okay, the man expressed his appreciation and stepped out of the truck.

I focused my attention on the wife. I took a set of vitals and explained that her husband's burns weren't serious. I shared about the common bond her husband and I had as pastors. As we talked, her anxieties slowly subsided and a new peace came over her. It was "that peace that transcends all understanding and is able to guard your hearts and minds in Christ Jesus." (Philippians 4:7). We shared a few minutes of fellowship and I spoke of the many possibilities that could have been.

"I know this is a great loss and disappointment," I said sincerely. "But you could have been on the trip when the fire occurred, or worse yet, your husband could have started the motorhome, stayed inside without noticing the fire, and the fire could have consumed the motorhome with him in it! The Lord was definitely watching over you and your husband today."

Viewing the fire from a new perspective, she began to recall her blessings. When her daughter arrived, the woman, now calm and encouraged, turned to me and calmly and assuredly said, "I know God sent you here today!" Then she left.

I smiled, overcome by a realization that this was indeed a divine appointment.

I completed my paperwork, returned to the station, and reflected on the unusual day. I thought about how I had arrived at the station that morning prepared for action, how I had missed that earlier call by three minutes, how God had had another plan for me — mutual encouragement with a brother in Christ. Even though the morning had passed in tedious and boring tasks, God gave my assistants and me time to share and uplift each other. Then came the fire, out of our normal response area, where my EMT was assigned to hose duty and I to seemingly minor medical assistance. But in that seemingly minor medical assistance, God knew a fellow brother and sister needed encouragement that day and so He directed my path once again. Praise God!

In Hebrews 10:25 God instructs us to encourage one another. This verse has special meaning for me in several ways. As a paramedic and firefighter I, like all those in this profession, witness destruction, tragedy, loss, and emotional stress on a regular basis. Whether it be the loss of possessions or the loss of life, at times the heartache is unbearable. That's when I turn to my Lord and Savior. In all His awesome and majestic glory, He strengthens and comforts me. Many times His strength and comfort come from the encouragement of a fellow believer that God placed specifically in my path.

Hebrews 10:25 also has special meaning for me because it is the key verse adopted by the Fellowship of Christian Firefighters, an organization dedicated to bringing encouragement to fire service personnel internationally, to glorifying God, and to sharing the Good News of Jesus Christ.

I am honored to be president of the Treasure Coast Chapter in St. Lucie County, Florida and I thank God for the Christian firefighters and paramedics that I work with. When tough calls occur, God consistently places someone close by. There is nothing like having a brother or sister in the Lord nearby when encouragement is needed. And believe me, in this business encouragement is needed a lot.

A LIGHTER MOMENT

"There is an appointed time for everything . . ."

Get Out Of The Way Rico

It was not unusual to see Rico Pockard staggering around the higher crime areas of our district, interfering with law enforcement or fire-rescue personnel in the course of their duties. He seemed to have a keen sense when it came to locating the scene of an emergency. Rico was an alcoholic street person who was notorious for actually stepping out onto the street and directly into the paths of fire, rescue, and police personnel while they responded to calls with lights and sirens. He would actually hinder progress until someone gave him a quarter or a cigarette. Then, and only then, would he move. Even trips to jail didn't seem to change his ways.

Stories — such as the one that happened to me regarding Rico — were frequently told and retold in amusing conversations at the station.

We responded to an elderly lady's house — "a possible stroke." It was only 11:00 in the morning. We arrived, stopped at curbside, and began to approach the house. We looked up and there was Rico in his usual intoxicated state, hanging around the intersection a block away. No doubt, when he heard the sirens, he anticipated his golden opportunity for a handout from the fire-rescue guys. He probably thought he was especially lucky because he didn't even have to flag us down in traffic — we had already stopped and were easily accessible.

Paying no attention to him, we proceeded to the front porch and to our patient. She was sitting on a chair appearing conscious and alert. As we began to assess her condition and gather information about her medical problem, Rico boldly walked into this lady's front yard and up to her front porch.

"Oh no," I thought. "This lady's got more problems than she knows. She's got a guy hanging out in front of her house gawking while she is in a distressed condition."

I looked at David, the lieutenant in charge. Disgust registered in his eyes.

"Rico, go away," David firmly stated through the screened porch door.

Did Rico listen? Of course not. Not only did he not leave, but he then decided to open the porch door and invite himself in.

"You got a dollar?" Rico asked in response to being told to leave.

"No," David replied. "We have a patient here. Can't you see? This is serious business. Now leave."

Fortunately I was standing between our patient and David and Rico. I'm sure this lady couldn't believe some guy just came inside her house and asked the emergency personnel for a handout. Or perhaps she, too, knew Rico and therefore mentally brushed him and his behavior off as the Rico everyone knew.

Behind me, I continued to hear Rico and David talking. David was failing in his attempt to rid the porch of Rico. Finally, the clincher came when I looked around and heard David say, "Rico, just beat it!"

So what did Rico do? He started dancing around on this lady's front porch in his intoxicated state, singing the words to the popular Michael Jackson song, "Beat It."

I couldn't hold back my laughter despite my compassion for this poor lady. We knew further on-scene assessment was out of the question. We loaded her quickly into the unit. David escorted Rico back to the street. As we headed for the hospital, we dodged a dancing Rico at the end of the driveway. He just couldn't understand the meaning of the words "beat it," but he sure knew how to sing the song.

". . . A time to laugh."

ECCLESIASTES 3A: 1 AND 4B

CHAPTER 15

Why?

" 'For my thoughts are not your thoughts, neither are your ways My way,'" declares the Lord. "'For as the heavens are higher than the earth, so are My ways higher than yours and My thoughts than your thoughts.' "

ISAIAH 55: 8-9

Lauren, my five-year old daughter, sat at the end of the table playing contentedly with her "happy meal" toy. Sara and Luke, my other children, talked about the books they had checked out from the library. Between chats with the kids, Alicia and I talked about the day's activities. After dinner came baths and family time, followed by bedtime prayers and good-night kisses.

With the kids tucked into bed, I sat down to write. Glancing at the "happy meal" toy, my mind drifted once again to my children. "What precious gifts from God," I thought as a warmth came over me. I reflected upon their loving and trusting nature and realized how truly blessed I was because of them.

I rose and checked on them once more, then returned to my desk. With the vision of my children still vivid in my mind, I felt a tear form as I remembered the following calls — calls that pertain to the most difficult part of my job — dealing with little ones who are sick or injured. Even more heart-rending are the calls when God takes a little one home.

Every day I try to walk closely with God and to listen to

His voice. I have no doubt about His all-powerful, all-knowing, and all-loving nature. But I must realize that sometimes God chooses for us not to understand His reasons for allowing things to happen as they do. I know He has a plan for us, a plan far more wondrous than our human minds can conceive and yet, when I see a child face injury or death, my heart still cries out, "Why?"

I will never know the answer to many of the "Why's" in life, but I do know God is faithful and I can turn to Him for strength and peace. It is through Him, and only Him, that I find comfort in cases such as these that follow.

My first call concerning a child was for a young boy who was called home to be with the Lord. He was about my son's age, eight years old. While riding home on his bicycle he was hit by a car and suffered a fatal head injury. He died moments after we got him to the hospital. His little motionless body on the emergency room gurney left a deep impression on me. The other guys on the call with me didn't seemed phased. Didn't they care? Maybe they just didn't show their feelings. I don't know. What I do know is, I was hurting. I retreated to the dorm where sporadic tears fell onto my pillow. I honestly had doubts about continuing in this type of work. But praise God for His strength and comfort. How people can deal with tragedy without the Lord I'll never know.

Several months later I experienced the loss of another little one. An eight-month-old child got his head stuck between a broken bar of his crib and strangled to death. My heart and emotions raced as the grandmother, who was baby-sitting, ran a lifeless little body out to our arriving truck. For a futile hour and a half, our guys and the emergency room staff tried to bring life back to this little one. But the whole time, this little child was already giggling and smiling in the lap of his Heavenly Father. Moments later I was again crushed and broken as I walked by the family waiting room and saw a young mommy and daddy sobbing uncontrollably on each other's shoulders.

Unlike the first call, the guys with me on this second call

were visibly hurting. We talked. We questioned. We pondered — "What if?" We encouraged one another, we prayed, we cried, and we knew that the real source of strength was the common denominator of knowing God was in control, that God's ways are not our ways, and that God has a purpose for all things — a purpose we may never know or understand in this life.

Another unsettling call involving a child resulted in deepening the bond of friendship between my already close friend, David French, and me. David, more like a brother than a fellow worker, was saved as a teenager, drifted far away from the Lord, and had recently rededicated his life. God was working in his life and using me for spiritual encouragement. We often talked of God's goodness and the opportunities we had to witness His love on calls. Without question God placed us together for spiritual strength and comfort on this particular call.

David and I were stationed in the busiest station in the area. Even though we were both paramedics, I had recently been promoted to engineer and was assigned to the engine. He was assigned to the station's rescue truck. It was raining that day and the roads, including the fast-paced Florida Turnpike, were slick and slippery. All the conditions were prime for accidents. We anticipated a busy day, but nothing of the magnitude of what followed. A call came in for a van, carrying seven family members, that blew a tire. The driver lost control. The van skipped, flipped over numerous times, and landed upside down. Three people were ejected. Four were trapped inside.

We were the first trucks out. David and his crew, in the rescue truck, pulled easily away and were out of our sight within the first five miles of response. Our engine was governed for a top speed of sixty-five mph. I was pushing the pedal through the floorboard watching the mile markers go slowly by. It's embarrassing when a Volkswagen bug passes you by when you're responding Code 3! It's unnerving to know you are needed on scene and unable to get there any sooner. But, it is better to get there than to overheat and be useless, I reasoned.

We knew two more rescue trucks from other stations were en route and that Air One, our trauma helicopter, was dispatched and about twenty miles from the scene.

My lieutenant got on the radio. "Rescue 1, let us know what you have when you get there."

"10-4," Rescue 1 replied.

Florida Highway Patrol were first on scene. Dispatch relayed their update. This was without a doubt a high priority call.

Rescue 1 arrived. They quickly issued multiple trauma alerts, an automatic message to the base hospital that a patient in the field has suffered life-threatening trauma. In response to a trauma alert, the hospital goes on a state of readiness for receiving the trauma patient. We learned that there were a minimum of four trauma patients on this call.

Our engine was still three to four minutes away. David radioed us. He was working a two-year in critical condition that had been ejected from the van. In addition, ALS (advanced life support) was needed for at least three others. "Hurry up," he added as he hastily ended his transmission.

Dispatch notified us of a possible fuel leak. My lieutenant looked over at me and said, "Do your paramedic thing; we'll take care of fire concerns."

We arrived on scene amidst confusion, chaos, destruction, and loss. The van was crunched upside down into the median. A blood-stained sheet covered one body.

I went into action while surveying the scene and looking for my friend, David. I located him. He was in the back of Rescue 1. An emergency room nurse, who passed by after the accident occurred, was ventilating the young boy while David tried to get an IV into one of the child's neck veins.

I grabbed one of my crew members. We ran toward several other patients stationed near the van. A teenage girl was covered with roadrash and had apparent multiple fractures, but she was

Manglement and death are all too familiar in the field of fire rescue.

Photo courtesy of the Fort Pierce Tribune, Florida

breathing and awake.

Two other rescue trucks arrived and went to work on the remaining occupants trapped inside the van.

The southbound lane was cleared and Air One was given permission to touch down. After a secondary triage or assessment, it was decided that David and his patient would fly.

As we worked on another patient, I occasionally peeked into the back of Rescue 1, wondering if the little one David was working on was showing any response. Amazingly the father, and driver of the van, was unhurt physically and was standing at the back of the ambulance glaring intently at the efforts to revive his son. While my patient was being packaged onto the spine board and immobilized, I darted over and jumped into the back of Rescue 1.

"David, got any response?" I asked.

"No, not really — maybe a small attempt at respiration."

"They're about ready for you to load into the chopper," I stated as I jumped out through the back door.

Before heading back to my patient, I glanced at the child's father. "That's your son, isn't it?" I cautiously said.

He looked down sadly, nodded his head, and uttered, "Yes, that's my son."

"We're doing all we can for him, including praying. Will you pray, too?". I said compassionately. Then I returned to my patient.

Within minutes David and the child were airborne. Shortly thereafter my patient and the other occupants of the van were on their way to the hospital.

Despite desperate efforts on the part of David, his crew, and the ER staff, the little boy went on to be with the Lord.

We returned to the station and numbly got our equipment back in order. I was overwhelmed by the tragedy. I knew if I needed encouragement over dealing with this wreck, David certainly needed some, too. I went in search of my friend and found him in the dorm, sitting on his bunk.

"David, you did all you could," I calmly affirmed, placing my hand on his shoulder.

"Ya, but . . . why? Why the little one, Tommy?" he questioned, barely able to look me in the eyes.

"All I know, David, is that the Lord has little ones' that He specifically chooses to take home, and this was one of them. God's thoughts are not the same as ours, David. They are much higher, much purer. This child must be so precious to God that He called Him home early for a purpose we may never fully understand in this life. We just have to trust and believe."

It was a difficult time for both of us. We continued to share and encourage each other spiritually that night as well as on the many subsequent calls we have made together over the years.

Our bond of friendship continues to grow. There is nothing comparable to having a brother or sister in the Lord nearby when encouragement is needed. And believe me, in this business, one doesn't go very long without needing encouragement.

Sharing God's Word
Engineer Peter Morris, Paramedic Tommy Neiman, Firefighter Tom Bruhn, Lieutenant Mike Jenkins, and Firefighter Sam Gonzalez.

Photo courtesy of the Fort Pierce Tribune, Florida

CHAPTER 16

The Last Alarm

". . . that if you confess with your mouth, Jesus as Lord, and believe in your heart that God raised Him from the dead, you will be saved."

ROMANS 10:9

One of the primary fire service publications contains a section called "The Last Alarm." This special segment is devoted to the recognition and honor of those who recently died in the line of duty. An issue seldom passes without my looking over the names and departments where these firefighters answered their final calls. I think about their families, the children they left behind, and the people they worked with. Then I wonder, did these men and women know the Lord as their real and personal Savior?

Each month, as I look at the names of firefighters who answered their final calls, I pray for the families they left behind, the comrades they worked with, the friends and neighbors they associated with. I'm saddened as I think of the children and the void that a loss of a parent leaves in their lives.

God placed a heavy burden on my heart for my lost brothers and sisters in my own fire department, the departments around me, and for lost brothers and sisters in departments all over this nation. But the burden extends even further; it extends to all who are lost, who do not know Jesus, and consequently do not have the assurance that should their last alarm sound, they would spend eternity with Jesus.

In 1996, according to the National Fire Protection Association (NFPA), public fire departments responded to 1,975,000 calls. From 1977 to 1997 there were 2,471 firefighter fatalities. In 1997, involvement in emergency vehicle/motor vehicle incidents was the second leading cause of death, and nationwide someone died in a fire every 105 minutes. The figures continue in alarming numbers, but they are more than figures — each represents an individual occurrence and more importantly individuals themselves. Each is someone's child, parent, sibling, loved one, or friend.

A short while ago I was called to transport a twenty-six-year-old woman in the later stages of AIDS. Barely able to move, she collapsed trying to get up at her converted motel room apartment. Weighing less than fifty pounds, it was nothing to single-handedly place her on our stretcher. When I first looked into the room, I knew God had called our crew out of our normal zone and sent me to minister to this person.

The young lady was deathly weak and trembling throughout. I felt compelled not to waste one second of the five-minute ride to the hospital. I took her shaking hand and delicately but straightforwardly said, "Melissa, you know you haven't got long, don't you? Do you know Jesus loves you? Have you trusted Him to be your Savior?"

With a weak faint voice she nodded her head and said, "Yes." Fear still covered her trembling face.

Lowering myself from the bench seat and leaning close to her ear, I quietly said, "Melissa, you don't have to be afraid; Jesus is going to be right there holding you as you pass with Him into glory."

She smiled and closed her eyes as if immediately sensing His presence. I prayed with her and then reaffirmed the truth that God erased her past when she trusted the Lord in her heart. As she slipped from this world into eternity, I told her I would see her again someday because of what Jesus Christ did for us 2000 years ago.

Whether a fatal illness, an accident, the natural process of aging, or in the line of duty, all of us will someday encounter our "Last Alarm."

When your final alarm sounds, what will your destiny be?

The choice is up to you. God has already done His part — He sent His only Son to die on the cross for your sins. Christ has done His part — He came to earth in the form of man, died a brutal death on the cross, rose from the dead, ascended to heaven, and prepared a place for you in eternity with Him. The rest is up to you.

If you want to spend eternity with God, some simple steps to follow are on the next page:

SALVATION PRAYER

† **Realize you** (as all humans) **are a sinner:** "For all have sinned and fall short of the glory of God." (Romans 3:23).

† **Accept the free gift of God:** "The wages of sin is death (spiritual death); but the free gift of God is eternal life in Christ Jesus our Lord." (Romans 6:23).

† **Recognize that this gift is not earned or deserved:** "For by grace you have been saved through faith; and that is not of yourselves; it is the gift of God; not as a result of works so that no one may boast." (Ephesians 2:8,9).

† **Believe that Jesus Christ is the only Son of God sent by God to bear the burden of our sins:** "For God so loved the world (that's you and I), that He gave His only begotten Son, that whoever believes in Him shall not perish, but have everlasting life." (John 3:16).

† **Confess and believe that Jesus is God's only Son:** "...that if you confess with your mouth, Jesus is Lord, and believe in your heart that God raised Him from the dead, you will be saved." (Romans 10:9).

Pray:

Dear Jesus: I know that I am a sinner. I know You love me and You don't want me to be separated from You eternally. I believe You are the only Son of God and that You willingly died on the cross for my sins. I now repent of my sins and receive You as Savior and Lord of my life. Thank You for saving me and help me to live a life that is pleasing to You. AMEN.

If you just prayed this prayer, I want to be the first to congratulate you! The Bible tells us that there is rejoicing in heaven over one soul that trusts in Jesus. My prayer is that you will join other believers in a Christ-centered church where you can grow and learn more about this loving Savior that has come into your heart. If you are a firefighter, I suggest you contact the Fellowship of Christian Firefighters International, an organization that ministers to the fire service. The phone number is 1-800-322-9848.

And if you're already a child of this most loving Father, I hope this book has been a source of encouragement and strength in your walk with the Lord. If anything, as the cover of this book illustrates, I hope you'll realize that whatever fires you encounter, Jesus is right there with you!

God Bless You.

ORDER FORM

For additional copies of **Sirens For The Cross** or for information regarding booking Tommy Neiman for speaking engagements, contact:

Tommy Neiman
150 Woodcrest Dr.
Fort Pierce, FL 34945
Sirens4TC@aol.com
904-788-7177

OR

Embrace Communications and
Fellowship of Christian
Firefighters, International
6887 Red Mountain Road
Livermore, CO 80536
Fax : 970-407-0083
Phone: 1-800-322-9848
E-mail: fcfint@webaccess.net

- -

Please send ____ copies of **Sirens For The Cross** at $12.95 each plus $4.00 shipping and handling. Colorado residents please add 3.8 sales tax ($.49 each). Florida residents please add 6.5% sales tax ($.84 each).

Name: ____

Last First M.I.

Address: ____

City: ____________________ State: _____ Zip: _____________

Phone: (Day) _________________ (Evening) ________________

My payment is being made in the following way

☐ Check ☐ Money Order ☐ Visa ☐ Master Card

Name of Cardholder: ___________________________________

Signature: ____

Card Number: ___________________ Exp. Date: ____________